A SEASON OF MYSTERY

Other Books by Paula Huston

By Way of Grace: Moving from Faithfulness to Holiness

Daughters of Song

Forgiveness: Following Jesus into Radical Loving

The Holy Way: Practices for a Simple Life

Signatures of Grace: Catholic Writers on the Sacraments

Simplifying the Soul: Lenten Practices to Renew the Spirit

A SEASON OF MYSTERY

10 SPIRITUAL PRACTICES FOR EMBRACING A HAPPIER SECOND HALF OF LIFE

PAULA HUSTON

LOYOLA PRESS.
A JESUIT MINISTRY
Chicago

LOYOLAPRESS.
A JESUIT MINISTRY

3441 N. Ashland Avenue
Chicago, Illinois 60657
(800) 621-1008
www.loyolapress.com

Author's note: A couple of names and several details have been changed to protect the privacy of those I have written about.

All Scriptures, unless otherwise noted, are taken from the *New Revised Standard Version Bible: Catholic Edition*, copyright © 1980, 1993. Division of Christian Education of the National Council of Churches in the U.S.A. Used by permission. All rights reserved.

Art credit: Veer/Alloy Photography

Library of Congress Cataloging-in-Publication Data
Huston, Paula.
  A season of mystery / Paula Huston.
    p. cm.
  Includes bibliographical references.
  ISBN-13: 978-0-8294-3754-6
  ISBN-10: 0-8294-3754-1
  1. Middle-aged persons--Religious life. 2. Older Christians--Religious life. 3. Spiritual life--Catholic Church. I. Title.
  BV4579.5.H87 2012
  248.8'4—dc23

                                                        2012026229

Printed in the United States of America.
12 13 14 15 16 17 Bang 10 9 8 7 6 5 4 3 2 1

For Margaret Joy, sweet anam cara, 1927–2012

Contents

Arriving

I am studying a photo of my mom in Barcelona, a picture taken twenty-five years ago; in it she is the age I am now. A slim brunette sitting in the shadows of a Moorish hotel garden beside my handsome dad, she could be thirty-five, forty, or even a young fifty, but surely not what she actually is: about to begin her seventh decade. She has never been to Spain before. They are here to celebrate their anniversary, and there is no hint on her calm and happy face that within four years of this culminating moment, she will be a widow and that life will have changed forever.

Old age is a mystery. It steals in upon us and quietly relieves us of our youth and our beloveds. Once it has arrived, it stays, and the indelible marks of our decay begin to appear upon our faces. In its grip, our path starts to veer, and eventually we find ourselves standing before that daunting gateway called death. Whatever we have managed to hold on to during the silent struggle with aging must now be relinquished forever. Our time is up, our journey over. And, faith or no faith, what happens next is shrouded in obscurity.

Right now, I am my mom in Barcelona. At almost sixty, I can still pass for middle-aged, and it's easy to convince myself that what happened to her—early widowhood, a potentially lethal illness, the inexorable crumbling of her dark-eyed beauty—will never happen to me. After all, I am at the top of my game. I can still hoist a grandchild in each arm, write books, teach, jog, and backpack. I'm clearly too strong and healthy to get old, so what do I have to fear?

My culture heartily concurs and offers me two inspiring myths. The first is that technology is my friend, and if only I am willing to tap into its wondrous resources, I never have to age or die. The second myth is loftier and does not concern itself with wrinkle abatement; instead, it assures me that the older I get, the more fascinating, wise, and powerful I am destined to become.

The first myth, clearly corporate-sponsored, encourages me to spend a lot of money on health supplements, gym memberships, plastic surgery, and hormone replacement therapy. The second taps into my unrealized ambitions and leads me to seek gurus who can bring me forth into full blossom. Underlying each is the same unquestioned modern belief: the purpose of life is to get what I most want before I die. Postponing aging buys me the time to do that, and "believing in myself," as the gurus put it, provides the necessary inspiration.

If my culture is right about this—and it does make a passionate case for itself—then my job from now on becomes clear. I must avoid aging at all costs. I must live as though there is no death. And most of all, I must strive harder than I ever have before to achieve my unrealized aspirations, obtain what I desire but still lack, and come into my own as a self-fulfilled, autonomous being.

So why does such stirring rhetoric make me feel so tired?

One of the great minds of the twentieth century, philosopher and novelist Iris Murdoch, speaks of the consoling illusions we so readily embrace. Such fantasies make us feel better when we are hurting or even help us bear real suffering. They inspire us to higher purposes; they sustain us for the long haul. What then can be wrong with them? Her answer is simple: they shield us from the truth. And since we are truth-seeking creatures, ultimately such fantasies cannot satisfy.

If our two modern myths about aging are really just consoling illusions, then where can we find a more truthful view? If our culture's underlying belief about the purpose of life is misguided, then where shall we go for wisdom?

These questions are crucial, because if there is one thing I have learned from my mother's slow decline, it is this: old age is the most challenging stage of life we face. We must be able to tap into all the wonderment of childhood, the hope of young love, the patience of parenthood, and the determination of middle age if we are not to be defeated by it. Yet it is calling us to be better people than we've ever been, while at the same time, it is diminishing our capacities for serious effort. The irony of old age, which slowly reduces us to infancy, is that we must be true adults to survive it.

Right now I am my mom in Barcelona. In twenty-five years, if I am still here, I will be as gray and unsteady on my feet as she is rapidly becoming. My children will be trying their best to take the car away, to help me update my will, to get me into a senior residence where nurses can dole out my medications. I'll be wearing hearing aids and mixing up dates and forgetting to turn off the flame on the stove. No matter how much money I have spent on hormones and health supplements, no matter how many gurus I have consulted, I will be old.

And there's no getting out of it.

There is, however, a different way to face it. And there are at least three good reasons for doing so. The first is that we can avoid a lot of unnecessary brooding and unhappiness. The second is that we can live a better life. The third is that we can more easily prepare ourselves for death and what follows afterward.

The cultural belief that getting what we most want will make us happy is not a new one. It has cropped up regularly for millennia, and every time it does, it is disproved by the facts. Fabulously wealthy people—superstars and celebrities and CEOs—theoretically have the resources and freedom to obtain whatever they most desire. Yet they are famously dissatisfied, plagued by restless boredom as they endlessly seek what will finally bring them peace.

The rest of us, with fewer dollars or hours to spend on the quest, do not escape the suffering. We feel cheated out of what we deserve. We feel like failures. We become envious and resentful of those who have what we want. Equally dissatisfied, we are ripe for depression and anger, both of which get dramatically compounded when we face the inevitable losses of old age.

Setting aside the fruitless quest to get everything we want before we die, then, frees us up to become better human beings. Philosophers have long pointed out the difference between the "enviable" life and the "admirable" life. The first may be aesthetically tasteful and filled with interesting adventures: we keep a yacht in the Bahamas, climb Mount Everest, collect masterpieces, or make great wine. The second may be less pleasing, at least on the surface: we pour ourselves out in a Calcutta hospital for the dying, adopt a crack baby, take care of our Alzheimer's-stricken father for a decade before he dies.

Though the enviable life inevitably wins out in the sense that we find it the most enticing—who wouldn't choose Himalayan trekking over thankless caregiving?—it is the second kind of life that haunts us with its images of what we might become if only we had enough courage and faith. It is the difficult, admirable life that calls out of us what is highest and best and most satisfying.

Transcending the endless cycle of want-satisfaction also gets us ready for death and what follows. My friend Betty, age eighty-five, sums it up like this: "Getting old is about preparing for the next life. But nobody these days is thinking about that anymore."

Though recent polls indicate that most of us believe in some kind of afterlife, it's unclear by our behavior what this means or how this belief is being translated into the decisions we make here and now. As contemporary Christians, it seems that we are much more "this-worldly" than in previous eras. We believe it is good to focus on the present, to value the physical world, and to get the most out of living. Thus, we spend little time pondering Christ's words about what's to come.

Yet given the poignant nature of aging with all its griefs and losses, why do so many of us studiously ignore the most hopeful news we will ever get? That news is that Jesus has conquered death. He states, "I am the living bread that came down from heaven. Whoever eats of this bread will live forever" (John 6:51). What's more, we will not have to cart our deafness and varicose veins and dementia with us into the next life: "For we know that if the earthly tent we live in is destroyed, we have a building from God, a house not made with hands, eternal in the heavens" (2 Corinthians 5:1).

We won't have to sign up on any waiting lists to get into this fabulous new residence, for a room has already been set aside with our name on the door. Jesus assures us, "In my Father's house there are many dwelling places" (John 14:2). And lest we worry about being overlooked, he adds, "Are not two sparrows sold for a penny? Yet not one of them will fall to the ground apart from your Father. . . . So do not be afraid; you are of more value than many sparrows" (Matthew 10:29–31).

No need, it turns out, to spend thousands on pharmaceuticals. No need for Botox or slavish obedience to a personal trainer. Through Christ, we have been liberated from all fruitless efforts to artificially extend our physical lives. Through him, we have been freed from the grim quest to satisfy every desire.

So how shall we face old age and dying? We can set aside the comforting myths that tell us we can indefinitely postpone what's coming next. We can cease the frantic efforts to achieve all our unfulfilled goals before we die. Then we can move into this most challenging phase of life with both eyes open, remembering that our real purpose here on earth is to be "servants of Christ and stewards of God's mysteries" (1 Corinthians 4:1).

A Season of Mystery asserts that this second half of life brings on the "best of times and the worst of times," as my eighty-five-year-old friend Brother Emmanuel ruefully puts it. The losses are painfully real. But so are the opportunities, if only we can allow ourselves to let go of the myths. When we do, we open the door to genuine adventure, including some of the richest spiritual experiences we may ever have.

Each chapter in this book suggests a spiritual discipline that is particularly suited to the second half of life. The practice of listening, for example, helps us stop superimposing our own take on every situation before we even have a chance to hear and see what is really there. The practice of delighting encourages us to notice and be thankful for what is small and seemingly insignificant. The practice of generating teaches us how to sow seeds for the future in those who are much younger. Though each discipline stands on its own, it is also meant to be an antidote to the classic afflictions of curmudgeonly old age: close-mindedness, complaining, fear of change, obsessing about comfort and security, boredom, denial, resentment, judgmentalism, hoarding, and cursing an increasingly unfamiliar world.

None of these practices are about achievement. Nor is the goal self-improvement (it is very hard to teach old dogs new tricks, after all); but instead, they are about becoming "ordinary mystics." Theologian Karl Rahner uses this term to describe typical people—nobody special—who nevertheless live in the continual presence of God.[1]

One of the most beautiful teachings of Christianity, on par with the promise of everlasting life and an enduring relationship with God, is the assurance that we are never alone on this difficult earthly journey. Instead, we are part of a vast community, both living and dead, bound together with unbreakable ties of love. We face none of this alone.

I'm still at the beginning of this mysterious season. And I'm fortunate to have many friends who are much older than I am, some of whom have already passed on and others who are still living and available for consultation. I also have beloved friends who've reached old age well before their time, thanks to diseases such as Parkinson's and multiple sclerosis. In this book I'm leaning on their wisdom, along with the insights of great contemplatives and saints, from the fourth-century Diadochus of Photikë to the twentieth-century Henri Nouwen.

It is true: I *am* my mom in Barcelona, poised on the precipitous edge of a long decline. Am I nervous? Of course; none of us can ponder physical decay and its inevitable end without some healthy trepidation. To balk at this point, however—to go into denial and turn back toward the consoling illusions of our culture—would be self-defeating. Instead, I seek hope in the vision of an ancient Syrian monk, St. Ephrem of Nisibis:

Death becomes something new for those who
have died:
at it they have put off suffering,
and at it they put on glory.[2]

1
Listening

Thus, in the proper state we will know how faultlessly to recognize the word of God, if we spend hours in untroubled silence, not speaking and in the fervent memory of God.³
—Diadochus of Photikë (c. 400–487)

Around the time my parents were celebrating their anniversary in Barcelona, Mike and I were preparing to marry. We needed a place to raise four soon-to-be-reluctantly-yoked-together young step-siblings, and so we began hunting for some land. This was what we needed, we thought: a big project that would pull the six of us together. A place in the country, far removed from fast-food joints and shopping malls and video arcades—a peaceful, Amish-like sanctuary where a fragile new blended family might root itself and grow.

After weeks of searching, we finally found it. The lot was a sandy, weed-choked field shaded by a hill so steep you needed crampons to climb it, with a supremely ugly spec house hidden in one corner of the parcel by a shaggy grove of mastodon-sized eucalyptus trees. Its only virtue was that it was about to be foreclosed on, which meant we could afford it.

The sandstone hill was so deeply eroded we could park a pickup in the gullies, while the flat part of the acreage, festooned with humps of invasive pampas grass, became a mushy swamp during the lightest of rains. Manfully ignoring the obvious red flags (the kids

1

are going to *love* it here! just wait till we get horses!), we rolled up our sleeves and got to work.

We cleared and burned trailer-loads of brush, sawed down trees, broke up the hardpan, and dug postholes for a fence to protect what we romantically dubbed "Fox Hill Farm." We laid down irrigation systems, put up a barn, remodeled the house, planted orchards, excavated a pond, and constructed raised bed vegetable gardens—not to mention chicken coops, doghouses, rabbit pens, and swinging kitty doors.

The work was backbreaking, endless, and, because we were such amateurs, often had to be done over again. But we were so pleased with the results—our own olive oil, our own wine, our own eggs, our own honey! The story that had begun to write itself in our minds even before we moved onto the land grew ever more compelling.

As such stories often are, it was beautiful and poignant, showcasing our impressive creative gifts (so sadly squelched in those former marriages), our awesome love for one another, and our admirable enthusiasm for life. True, we had a history to overcome, but surely by now we had overcome it. And weren't the kids better off, divorces or not, because we had the courage to reach out and grab something more satisfying for us all?

In hindsight, it's quite clear that we were caught up in one of the consoling illusions Iris Murdoch describes. The hallmark of such lovely fantasies is their ability to close off other modes of perception. Everything is filtered through the lens of the story, which, because it is so intensely focused, has the power to generate prodigious amounts of creative energy. And then, like a perpetual motion machine, that energy gets used to act out story-generated compulsions.

The price of these sweet fantasies, however, is spiritual deafness. All we can hear is the sound of our own voice as it endlessly spins the fascinating tale of our exploits. The story itself serves to mask what's really going on, which is that our monumental efforts, no matter how noble-sounding, are more often than not about the same old quest: getting what we want.

What *did* we want? I believe that, along with the genuine respect for farming we both learned at the feet of our hardworking grandparents and the desire that our own children might get a taste of what we had experienced as kids on those family homesteads, we must have been longing for some kind of redemption—a redemption unconnected to the Christianity we had both abandoned.

At the time, I certainly couldn't make out what lay behind all that striving. Subterranean guilt? Worrying that we had put our kids in peril that far outweighed any of the benefits they were supposedly enjoying? It wasn't clear. But somehow our superhuman efforts to "make the desert bloom" seemed to cancel out these unacknowledged but vaguely troubling questions and make everything come out right.

Then I met a group of hermit monks whose lives of silence, solitude, and prayer both convicted me and showed me it was possible to change. Like the fourth-century desert fathers and mothers before them, the Camaldolese are a contemplative order, devoted to communion with God. Their daily work is prayer; all other enterprises, no matter how worthy, must give way before that primary imperative.

I fell in love with these monks, whose simple, peaceful lives seemed the antithesis of ours. I began making retreats at the Hermitage. I read about the ancient hermits of the desert, who took Christ's enigmatic words to the rich young man at face value: "If you wish to be perfect, go, sell your possessions, and give the money to the poor, and you will have treasure in heaven; then come, follow me" (Matthew 19:21). I came back to the faith, then to the church. In time, I made an oblate vow and became a lay member of the community. And though it took a while, Mike succumbed, too. Our old, familiar story began to lose its charm. The endless round of work began to slow.

But we still had our land, and even if we were no longer driven by that old, guilt-fueled creative vision, there remained lots to do. The kids grew up and went on to college, marriage, and parenthood. We both retired from our teaching careers but continued to carry on the many enterprises we had begun: pulling honey, making wine, harvesting olives for oil, growing fruits and vegetables. For one thing, all of this had cost us a ton in time and energy, so why abandon it now? For another, it seemed to be a particularly monastic way to live—off the land, through the labor of our own hands.

But then Mike began gently to complain, though not, for a while, in words. First, he began to limp. "My knee," he explained, when I finally asked. Several months after the operation to repair his torn meniscus, he started wandering the house at night, opening and closing the freezer door at 3 a.m. His thumb joint was failing, and only ice packs helped. The same surgeon fashioned him a whole new body part.

Then the sciatica started with an ominous shooting pain down one leg that ended in numb toes. The back doctor told him he needed to give the inflammation a chance to calm down, take a break. Take a break? Really? With all we had to do each day?

For a time, I clung to the belief that my longtime partner was just going through a string of bad luck. He'd always been so young and healthy for his age. And rather than feeling properly awed and grateful about that, I'd come to depend on it, as though his vim and vigor were in everlasting supply, as though he'd never, like any normal man in his late sixties, begin to show signs of wear and tear. I couldn't face the fact of his inevitable slowdown. If the truth were known, I'd have much preferred for him to stay thirty-four—the age he was when we first met and I fell in love with him.

Poor man. As the ailments piled up with almost no corresponding diminishment in the daily workload, he began to grow quiet and sad. After a long day of chores, he'd be too tired to eat much for dinner. Shortly thereafter, I'd find him in his big blue chair, asleep. Always a sociable guy, he became disturbingly reclusive almost overnight (or at least this is how it seemed to me, who by now was assiduously tracking his behavior).

It was time to see my friend Margaret Joy, who adores Mike and never fails to ask about him. Margaret is eighty-four and lives on her own in a small house on a large property occupied by a family with several teenage kids, who all love her and periodically knock on her door to ask her for advice. She likes being near young people. She tells me that they are very sweet, especially the boys, who never know how to say what's really on their minds. But Margaret also prizes her solitude, which has been hard-won and the result of not simply circumstance but a spiritual choice.

We sit down in her small living room under the butterfly tapestry on the wall. Margaret loves butterflies, which she takes to be earthly representations of angelic beauty. We sip our ginger tea.

"So how is *Mike*?" she asks, as I have hoped and expected that she will. I tell her I'm a wee bit concerned about him. I tell her that he is peckish and not himself these days—actually, somewhat wan and listless and seemingly defeated. I share that no matter how I've pondered the situation, I really don't have a clue what's going on with him. She listens with concern, her narrow, elegant face tipped a little, the mug of tea balanced on her knees. The butterflies dance on the wall behind us.

"And so," I finish with a flourish, "I'm really sort of stumped. And I have to say, I'm worried." At this, my eyes unexpectedly fill with tears.

Margaret says, "Oh, honey." She reaches out and pats my hand. Then she says, "I'll be praying for him. You tell him that, all right? I just love that man."

"I do, too," I say, gulping back more unexpected tears. What in the world is going on here? I've watched Mike suffer through his various injuries and inflammations for a while now. I've watched him slowing down and growing more tired and discouraged, but I've never felt like crying in front of him. What have I done instead? Given him bucking-up sorts of pep talks. I've tried to increase his enthusiasm level with my own bounciness, tried to keep our life on the land—the life we worked so hard to build—from slipping through our aching fingers.

"Thank you, Margaret," I say. "I'll tell him that." And this is the end of our conversation about Mike, except that it has given me an idea. I decide that, while Margaret is praying for him, I will be praying for him, too. I will drop my cheerleader efforts and pray instead.

Later that same afternoon, I ask Margaret about her own life, how things are going now that she's eighty-four instead of eighty-three or, for that matter, still seventy. Will she be able to stay in her little place, does she think? Doesn't she get lonely at times?

"Sometimes," she says matter-of-factly. "I mean, sometimes I can go for a few days without the phone ringing or someone knocking on the door. And I don't go out much, so there are long stretches of aloneness."

"That doesn't bother you?"

"Not really," she says. "I chose this, after all."

I nod. She did. I remember. "But what do you do with your time?" I ask. "During those days when nobody comes by?"

She laughs, her own chuckling-brook Margaret-style laugh, the one that validates her interesting middle name of "Joy," and says, "Mostly, I just listen."

I give her a sideways look. Like me, Margaret is a monastic oblate and steeped in the literature of contemplation, so I'm pretty sure I know what she is talking about. But unlike her, I've never experienced long periods of solitude and silence. Unlike her, I've never spent whole days in uninterrupted prayer.

She says, "It's sort of hard to describe. But really, it's just making myself available to what comes. It's an odd thing. You're just . . . there, without any expectations or strong desires. You're open. You're waiting. And then things do come, and they can be so unexpected. And you know you didn't make them up because you couldn't have. And at times they're very funny."

"How so?"

"Again, hard to describe, but what you're getting is such a different perspective. You're not used to seeing this way, and it's surprising. There's a kind of delight in it that you wouldn't get if it came from you."

"So, what you are saying is that you are getting *access* to something that's usually not available."

She thinks for moment, then smiles. "Yes, that's it in a nutshell."

When I leave Margaret, I am in a pensive mood. *Listening*. Or as Jesus puts it, "Let anyone with ears listen!" (Matthew 11:15).

The fifth-century Greek monk and bishop, Diadochus of Photikë, devoted much of his thinking to the problem of spiritual blindness and deafness. Though we are created in the image and likeness of God, though we are meant to perceive his presence in the very air we breathe, we lost this capacity when we chose to go our own way, leaving God behind. Our senses, once unified and focused on discerning what Diadochus refers to as the "footprints of the Invisible One" in our everyday lives, are now fragmented.[4] Our focus is shattered.

Diadochus believed that if we are willing to undergo *ascesis* (practice spiritual disciplines of renunciation), we can, through grace, be freed from the distractions that stop up our ears and blind our eyes. We can cease to impose limiting perceptual screens over life (grand stories about our own noble motives, for example) and in their place, recover *aisthesis*, "the lone sense that orient[s] the entire person through unmistakable perception of God."[5] My friend Margaret's daily, sustained practice of listening is her way of developing aisthesis.

Diadochus warned, however, that the difficulties of aging—the fear and worry they inspire, the sense of grief and loss, the temptation to cling to youth—can derail our best efforts to become spiritually unified beings.

> When we let ourselves get excessively upset on account of bodily irregularities that can befall us, we should realize that our soul is still enslaved by the desires of the body. Thus desiring material well-being, she refuses to separate herself from the material things of this life, considering it a great loss that, on account of illness, she no longer can enjoy the springtime of youth.[6]

Yet this mysterious season of aging is meant to be a time of preparation for the life to come. When we refuse to acknowledge that it has arrived, whether for ourselves or for a beloved spouse, as in my own case, we miss out on that precious opportunity. If on the other hand, we can accept what is going on, then we can take some practical steps to increase our capacity for listening.

What are these? First, we can consciously surrender up as many of our worries and plans as possible. These only clutter the airwaves. Second, we can deliberately focus on the present moment rather than on the future, concentrating on what is happening before our eyes rather than on what we hope will happen instead. Third, we can try our best to recognize the constant themes that keep running through our life; chances are, we have written this story ourselves, and it doesn't necessarily bear much relationship to reality. To be able to listen with spiritual ears, we have to set aside this self-created tale and simply wait for what comes next.

After my talk with Margaret Joy, I began to watch Mike in a different way, consciously trying to set aside worry and frustration over his diminishing energy and painful joints and looking instead with something closer to curiosity. Clearly, he was entering a new phase, and connected as we were, so was I. What awaited him? What would he have to teach me about growing older? Most of all, would the loss of that once formidable willpower translate into a greater openness to God's invisible presence in our lives?

It is still too early to tell. But unlike the days in which we blindly tried to impose meaning and purpose on our lives through sheer hard work, unable to hear any voice but our own, there is now a chance that God will speak and we will be able to hear him. As Trappist monk Thomas Merton says:

> To find the full meaning of our existence we must find not the meaning that we expect but the meaning that is revealed to us by God. The meaning that comes out of the transcendent darkness of his mystery and our own. We do not know God and we do not know ourselves. How then can we imagine that it is possible for us to chart our own course toward the discovery of the meaning of our life?[7]

There is only one way to do this. "Listen! I am standing at the door, knocking," says Jesus. "If you hear my voice and open the door, I will come in to you and eat with you, and you with me" (Revelation 3:20). The implication is, of course, that here, at the long-awaited banquet, the mystery of who we are will finally be revealed.

2
Delighting

*Sometimes when a farmer is looking for a suitable spot in
which to plant a tree, he unexpectedly comes across a treasure.
Something similar may happen to the seeker after God.*[8]
—Maximos the Confessor (c. 580–662)

As our children hit their late teens and began to move out into the
world, I found myself suffering through the classic empty-nest syndrome. They were *gone*, the kids we'd worked so hard to raise with
love despite the complicated stepfamily situation. They were grown
and gone, and we were finally on our own, a state I had longingly
dreamt of during those harried years of parenting.

Rather than feeling joy in this newfound freedom, I suffered
through a brief spell of loneliness, trying and failing to be brave. I
shed some tears. I tried to articulate the problem but couldn't put
it into words, except to say that it felt as though we'd just slipped
through a passageway I'd never seen coming. And there was no
going back.

We were very lucky; this time in our lives happened to fall during the economic boom that preceded the Great Recession, when it
was still possible for two schoolteachers to retire early and have some
adventures before the onset of old age. To counteract my droopiness,
we got busy doing the things that middle-aged empty-nesters used to
be able to do: we quit our jobs, we packed up the old camper called
"Turtle," and we took long road trips around the United States.

We made a long-dreamed-of trip to Europe, and we socialized with friends. And for a few years, life felt as open and free as it had been in early adolescence. While the kids were graduating from college, getting their first jobs, finding their mates, and marrying, we were as footloose as a couple of teenagers.

During this time, my mother-in-law, Mary, was briefly in the hospital for a benign but persistent arrhythmia. While trying to get out of bed, she fell and hit her head on the concrete floor, and within five hours had undergone brain surgery for a massive sub-dural hematoma. As suddenly as it had begun, our unexpected second adolescence was put on hold. My in-laws lived twenty minutes away from us, and we were the only family members close enough to be of any help.

A few days before Christmas, her hair grown out an inch and beginning to cover the huge incision scar, Mary was released from the rehab center to come home. Persistent swelling in the brain—an after-effect of the surgery—threw off her balance, scrambled her thinking, and sometimes gave her long, novelistic hallucinations from which it was impossible to extract her.

Our job was to keep her from trying to stand; standing was almost guaranteed to send her crashing over backward. Yet she could not be persuaded to stay put. Or if she was persuaded, at least for the moment, she could not be trusted, for almost immediately she forgot what she had just promised, forgot why she was sitting in that particular chair in that particular spot, forgot that she'd just come home from brain surgery and that things would never again be the same.

My first response to our new life situation was generous enough. I *wanted* to be able to help my in-laws, people whom, in my guilt over the divorces, I'd once mistrusted and avoided and assumed were judging me. But soon I found myself sinking into a funk. When was my father-in-law going to face reality? Bud was older than Mary, and he had no business trying to bathe and dress her, trying to cook for her or steady her at night during her countless trips to the bathroom. Tough Scotsman he might be, but the task was beyond him, and so, increasingly, he leaned on us for help.

As the weeks wore on, we continued to put in our shifts. I began to mutter my complaints to Mike, quietly at first ("Why can't he see they need some hired help around here?"), and then more vociferously ("It's only a matter of time till she falls again and breaks something or has to go through another brain surgery!").

These were not my only concerns, however. What was really on my mind I could not even say out loud. That even with all our good care, Mary might live on for years and years in this semicrippled, semibaffled, semipsychotic state. Were Mike and I really expected to sacrifice our hard-earned retirement on this altar of family duty?

Fortunately, my secret resentment did not extend to Mary herself. At times I gazed at her in wonder, trying to imagine myself confined to a living-room chair, the endless hours broken only by precarious trips down the long hallway to the toilet. In many ways, she was a genuine marvel, this mother of five sons, this small bird with broken wings.

In the middle of the unfolding Mary saga, our first grandson, Benjamin, was born. Our son called in the wee hours of the morning to tell us that our daughter-in-law was in labor. We packed the car and drove the three and a half hours to the hospital, stopping on the way only to pick up my mother, who was about to become a great-grandma. We arrived an hour before Ben did.

When the nurse brought the happy news, we rushed to the hallway and stood pressed up against the long nursery window, oooing and aaahing and pointing as they wheeled in his bassinet. He was sleeping, no doubt exhausted from surviving labor and delivery. An elfin blue cap covered his head. We could just make out his long dark lashes and a miniature curled fist.

Ben's birth was followed four months later by Eli's birth in New Mexico. Equally thrilling; equally instantaneous love. We were grandparents now, truly and irrevocably, and the gate that had begun to close with Mary's fall quietly clicked shut forever. Our mid-life adolescence was over, and our new role was clear. We who had been freed up from daily jobs were still strong and healthy enough to be of good use—we were to provide what our anxious, failing parents and our frazzled, overworked children, now parents themselves, could not muster up on their own behalf.

I am sitting on a bench overlooking the Pacific, trying to explain all this to a lifetime monk who got the call so young he never even had time to date before entering the seminary. Father Bernard and I go way back. He was the first monk I ever met, the first priest I ever confessed to, the first genuine hermit (for the Camaldolese are an eremitical order) with whom I ever had a conversation. He is also French Canadian, a linguistic fact intensified by the onset of Parkinson's disease a few years before. At five-foot-two-inches, with his snowy hair covered in a jaunty black beret and his mild, watery blue eyes covered by big lenses that could use some washing, he perches beside me like a wise old gnome, doing his best to follow the intricate family dynamics I am describing.

"And so," I finish, "though I dearly love them all, especially the grandkids, it's sort of scary to find myself playing this pivotal role in everybody's life right now. I didn't expect it. I wasn't prepared for it. I always thought the golden years were about . . . well, I don't know. But not about *this*."

"Pivet? Pivet?" The black beret is cocked in my direction. I'm not sure whether he hasn't heard me, hasn't understood me (even after all these years in an English-speaking country, he gets idiomatically confused at times), or is simply struggling with the Parkinson's again.

"*Piv*otal," I stress. "You know, as in essential. Crucial. Critical. As in, if I'm not there, everything falls apart."

I glance at him to see if he is now getting it, but he is back to staring at the ocean. For a while we sit in silence, as is our longtime habit. Then he announces, "One time I made friends with a what-do-you-call-it. A blue jay."

I wait. Finally, "You did?"

"He used to come to the window of my cell and look at me. His eye was very bright." I can see that, beneath the shadow of the black beret, he is smiling reminiscently, and I wonder what, if anything, this has to do with my family responsibilities. In the old days, before the Parkinson's, an apparent digression would eventually (though it sometimes took a long time and involved multiple further side-trails) connect back to the main point. Usually in a koan-like but incisive way that always made me laugh out loud. I don't know whether, at eighty-one, he still has it in him. Then he adds, "We enjoyed each other's company."

"I can imagine," I say. "Everybody enjoys your company. But what happened next?"

He smiles again. "I made a terrible mistake. I began to look upon him as you would a cat or a very small dog."

"You began to feed him."

He nods.

"Aren't there rules here against pets?"

"I broke them."

I laugh. "What happened next?"

"After a week, I had an attack of conscience. I explained to my friend that I could no longer carry on this relationship. No more food."

"How did he take it?"

"Not well. The next time I came out of my cell to go to Lauds, he flew down and landed on my head. When I told him good-bye, that the relationship was over, he pecked me very hard. I bled on my white robe." At this, Fr. Bernard pulls off the beret and points to a spot in the pink part of his snowy hair. "Is there a scar?"

I look carefully. There is nothing, though I do not doubt that the story unfolded exactly as he described. I shake my head. "Sorry. No scar." I wait for more—I wait for the point of the story and how it connects with my long litany of family responsibilities—but that's it. Fr. Bernard has bestowed on me his "little word," as the monastic tradition would call it, and it's up to me to figure it out.

As we shuffle back up the road to the Hermitage, he does add one more thing, seemingly unrelated. "Father Prior is a very good mother." Bernard in his old-fashioned way always refers to the prior of the community by his formal title. What he means, I think, is that the prior has shown him great tenderness and commitment during his recent hospitalization. That the sick and infirm always get top billing with Fr. Prior. And that Fr. Bernard, befriender of volatile blue jays, is both moved by and thankful for this loving, consistent support.

~~~~

If life's purpose lies in getting what we want, as our culture insists, then freedom becomes a very big deal. Freedom, we think, is what allows us to exercise our "inalienable right" to the pursuit of happiness. With this view of freedom, it's easy to feel threatened by constraint. Our instinct is to resist it with all our might, for it impedes our ability to live the life we think we want.

Yet to maximize this kind of freedom requires that we minimize or even eliminate serious relationships. For the more we rely on others or others rely on us, the less free we are to go wherever we wish to go, pursue whatever we wish to pursue, and do whatever we wish to do. Love constrains us. And in a society devoted to personal self-fulfillment, the cost of love often seems too high.

Surprisingly, freedom is a very big deal in the Gospels, too. However, here it means something quite different from what it means in twenty-first-century America. When Jesus says that "the truth will make you free" (John 8:36), he does not mean free to pursue personal happiness. When St. Paul says that it is "for freedom Christ has set us free" (Galatians 5:1), he does not mean we now have permission to satisfy our every impulse and whim. Quite the contrary. In the Bible, the "free" person is the one no longer plagued by the burdensome quest for money, pleasure, possessions, social status, and political power—the very things that our culture says will satisfy our deepest wants and make us happy.

Monks pursue this second kind of freedom by withdrawing from society with its antithetical view of what constitutes the good life. Though it appears that in so doing they escape the constraints imposed by serious relationships—they do not marry or have children, after all—community life requires equal self-sacrifice and love. Hence, in Fr. Bernard's words, Fr. Prior becomes a "good mother." Strangers become brothers. In monastic tradition, real love transcends personal preference; the truly free person is the one who loves as Christ loves.

The seventh-century Orthodox monk and mystic St. Maximos the Confessor shows us what this love looks like in real life:

> For him who is perfect in love and has reached the summit of dispassion there is no difference between his own or another's, or between Christians and unbelievers, or between slave and free, or even between male and female. But because he has risen above the tyranny of the passions and has fixed his attention on the single nature of man, he looks on all in the same way and shows the same disposition to all.[9]

He who loves as Christ loves, says Maximos, is not swayed by other people's characters. He does not love one person and hate another or, worse, "sometimes love and sometimes hate the same person."[10] He does not dwell on what pleases or repulses him in other people; he does not "split up the single human nature."[11] Instead, he "loves all men equally."[12]

This kind of indiscriminate love, falling on others like the rain that falls on both the good and the evil, is not driven by free personal choice in the modern sense but by something far deeper—enormous gratitude for life and for God's loving providence.

The result? We become capable of indescribable delight that "knows no bounds"; we "ceaselessly delight in divine beauty."[13] When we give up the personal quest for happiness so that we might embrace the constraints of love instead, then life with all its sorrow, sin, and suffering becomes inescapably delightful.

This means what? We can no longer predict how life's circumstances will come across to us or how we will react. We enter a state of near constant surprise and are jolted out of our torpid self-satisfaction by little shocks of joy.

Fr. Bernard's reminiscent smile when he told me the story of the vengeful blue jay is typical of those who see the world with this kind of holy delight. Everything—even a peck on the head—becomes an occasion for thanksgiving at the exuberant vitality of God's creation. And we do not have to become monks or even particularly holy in order to begin delighting in the world this way. But to do so, we must first give up our notions about what should or should not be. We must be willing to let go of personal preference or too much concern about what might inconvenience us. We must resist becoming anxious when things don't go our way. For an overly controlling stance is the enemy of delight.

My post-surgical mother-in-law was released from the rehab center three days before Christmas. To prepare for her arrival, we put up a tree, cleaned and decorated the house, and baked cookies. She'd been away from home for so long we were a little uneasy about how she might take it.

As it turned out, she took it very well. She seemed happy to be back, even if she was now confined to a chair. She was appreciative and complimentary. I, on the other hand, was a nervous wreck. I was nervous about helping her down the hallway to the bathroom, nervous about the possibility of her falling, nervous about what was to become of Mike and me, completely unqualified yet locked into this caregiving job with no end in sight.

I helped Mary into bed and pulled the blankets over a body made wraithlike by affliction. Her eyes were closed, and I thought she'd already dozed off when suddenly she murmured, "I need an enema. Could you give me one of those?"

"Oh, gosh, Mary," I stammered. "Gosh, I don't think so. I mean, I've never . . ."

"Don't worry," she said serenely, eyes still closed. "I can tell you how. I was a nurse, remember?"

And so, fumbling and caught between horror and hysterical laughter, I did it. I gave her that enema, for which she returned a dignified thanks. I went home and told Mike about it, and he told me I was a hero because neither he nor Bud could have pulled it off, and I began to think of myself, reluctantly but also rather proudly, as having become a *pivotal* person in Mary's rigidly curtailed existence. Maybe even a modest form of hero, just as Mike had said. In any event, I was sacrificing an awful lot—an *awful* lot—to remain loyally by her side through this long siege.

The next day I was helping Mary down the hallway, and we passed the half-open bathroom door. She glanced at the big rubber enema bag hanging from a towel rack and said blithely, with an insouciant half-wave, "There's our little friend." Suddenly, in the midst of all my high and self-important drama, we were laughing at the rubber bag.

I was catching a glimpse of the delight that is possible—only possible—when we steer ourselves away from what we think we deserve, what we think we need to be happy, what we call our precious freedom, and look at life through eyes of love.

3
Lightening

Let us, who are on the way, hasten home; for our whole life is like the journey of a single day. Our first duty is to love nothing here; but let us place our affections above, our desires above, our wisdom above, and above let us seek our home.[14]
—*Columban (c. 559–615)*

The crisis hit me during one of those neo-adolescent road trips before my mother-in-law's fall. A long-suppressed urge to downsize suddenly demanded a response. We were wandering the southwest part of the United States in "Turtle," our '73 Ford pick-up and '67 camper combo, and suddenly, as though scales were falling from my eyes, I saw clearly that I could live this way. Or rather, *we* could live this way, I breathlessly announced to Mike. So what if Turtle is old and beat up and leaky? What more do we need? And I gave him one of my glittering, deeply enthusiastic looks, the kind he's (rightly) learned to fear over the years.

"Hmm," he said carefully.

"But don't you see? Everything's so *simple* this way. At home we've got all that *stuff* to deal with."

"And? So?"

"So, why don't we just get rid of it all? Take up life on the road?"

"Well, we've had a good time in Turtle" (he was humoring me; I could hear it), "and there's a lot to take care of at home—that's true. But what about your garden? You love your garden."

"I do," I said, "but still . . ."

"And the cats," he added. "And the dogs and the chickens and the fruit trees and the olive trees and your writing studio."

"But . . ."

"And cooking for friends. And the kids. Don't forget the kids."

Jackpot. For much as I'd been enjoying this childless, responsibility-less interlude in our busy life, I'd not yet stopped missing those kids, grown and gone as they all were by now. And surely someday there would be grandkids too—I could almost see what they'd look like if I squinted my left eye. How would our offspring and their future families ever spend quality time with us if we took up permanent residence in Turtle?

"Well, couldn't we visit them instead? Wherever they wind up living?"

He gave me a look. One of our children was currently residing in an eight-by-ten-foot cabin in the middle of Nowhere, Central Oregon. Another was living in a converted attic in inner-city Newark, New Jersey. The third was spending some quality time in northern Norway. And the fourth had just moved back in with Mike's ex, who, even though she had plenty of room for Turtle in her driveway, was probably not going to be up for an extended visit from the likes of us.

And thus life in a 1967-era camper was struck from our list of possible options. But the urge to downsize—which had taken on a particular shape during my first visits to the monastery, but which had been bugging me for a long time before that—did not diminish. Periodically it came raging back at inopportune moments. When we arrived at a family reunion in the Colorado Rockies and were assigned our very own tiny and completely authentic log cabin, I refused to leave it for the next three days while the festivities went on without me. Back home, I began running free ads for priceless family artifacts such as the Mike-built bunk-bed set, the Cabbage Patch dolls, and the ancient but still living goldfish (plus bowl) that one of the kids had triumphantly borne home from the fourth-grade carnival a decade and a half before. Our far-flung brood became *really* outraged, however, when they heard I off-loaded our blue cockatiel at a local laundromat ("You sold *Petri*? Mom, we've had him for fourteen years!"). My increasingly urgent need for simpler, fewer, and less was adversely affecting my most important relationships.

What was going on here?

Some of it, I'm sure, was an overdue reaction to the creative excesses of the past. We'd worked so hard, spent so much, and sacrificed our strongest, healthiest years to that grand, misguided vision of "making the desert bloom" as compensation for breaking up two families in order to be together. The loss of that comforting illusion had taken some of the steam out of me. But this alone could not explain the persistent, almost painful, urge to lighten up.

It took a while to grasp the second major reason for all this *sturm und drang*— I received a big biological wake-up call via the onset of menopause. Though I was still relatively young at the time—only in my mid-forties—the symptoms were unmistakable. And with those physical signals came an almost primitive impulse to scatter and destroy the empty nest. My baby-making days were over. Finis. *Why waste time in sentimental tears?* I asked myself, taking note that my internal voice was a tad harsh these days. But it felt better to divest myself of all those ties to a now-dead past than to cling to physical reminders of what could never be again.

Our son Johnny, who had studied in India but was now teaching in Newark, helpfully pointed out to me: "You're in your Forest

Dweller stage, Mom. You're *supposed* to be leaving it all behind and going out to the woods with nothing."

"I am?"

He nodded sagely. "I'm still in the Student stage. And after that, I'll be in the Householder stage. But you're done with all that now, which is probably why you're acting crazy. You know, selling Petri to some random laundromat. Giving away the fish." He shook his head.

"Son," I said, tears springing to my eyes. "I am so, so sorry about that."

"No worries. We all get there someday, right?"

I have come to believe that we do get there, and the ancient Hindu wisdom about life's stages might serve us better at this time of life than most of what contemporary Western culture has to offer, such as cosmetic surgery and self-fulfillment seminars. Traditional Indian culture, which, these days, is rapidly giving way to Western modernism, allowed people a significant chunk of time for serious spiritual seeking. Men and women of the grandparent age were expected to leave behind their family responsibilities, divest themselves of their hard-earned possessions, and go out into nature to meet God. For if not then, when? Before this stage, one's energy is completely taken up with establishing an adult identity, whatever that may entail: going to school, obtaining training in a skill, acquiring a spouse or building a satisfying life as a single person, buying a house, working to support children or other relatives, meeting career-related goals.

I am convinced that the contemporary "mid-life crisis," which so often leads to flashy red Ferraris, hair transplants, and adultery, is actually a spiritual crisis in disguise. Suddenly, we can no longer abide our lives as they are. We become restless, irritable, irrational.

We want something, and we want it very badly, but we cannot name what *it* is. And so we grab at anything that will make us feel vibrant and alive again. Without a Forest Dweller tradition to steer us in the right direction, we completely fail to see what's afoot: that we're being called to strip down, to relinquish the responsibilities of middle age, and to seek until we finally find. The mid-life crisis hits at exactly the time we are meant to begin preparing for death. It offers what may be our last chance to face this reality with all our faculties intact.

Unfortunately, we get little backup from our society in this endeavor. Instead, we are urged to acquire more and to want more than it is even possible to acquire. However, there are some practical steps we can take to break this cycle, beginning with an honest assessment of our possessions. Are our houses cluttered with too many items? Do we have a storage unit we never visit? Have we stuck things away we can't even find? Is our habit to buy more supplies, whether these are food items, clothes, or other necessities, without even checking to see what we've already got on hand?

When we've taken a good hard look at our habits of acquisition, we can then begin to cull. But this works only if we make a pledge to ourselves not to buy anything new until we have truly gone through and disposed of what we already have. If the goal is a simpler, less cluttered life, then we must begin with how we spend our money.

Once I labeled myself an American Forest Dweller, I stopped trying to resist the troublesome urge to lighten up. I gave away clothing. I gave away books. I gave away furniture and kitchenware and artwork. I gave away old, outdated stuff, but I also gave away perfectly good, practically new items, often gifts. And the more I gave away, the calmer I became. Deep inside, though, I still longed for that tiny cabin in the Rockies, or even the long-departed Turtle.

Then came an opportunity we'd been waiting for: the chance to build a second home on our four acres. We told people it was a "retirement" home; really, it was just a simpler, smaller house with lots of windows and hardly any storage space, where we'd be forced to hold at bay the temptation to acquire. By the time we moved into our 925-square-foot living area a year and a half later, we had stripped down to the basics. And finally, this painful business of lightening, which had caused me so much stress and trouble, came undramatically to its natural end. It seemed that I had solved the conundrum of what one does with the accumulated memories of a lifetime. It seemed that I'd found the right direction, tough as it had been, and I felt pretty darn pleased with myself for that.

For the moment, at least.

Jesus speaks often about our peculiar propensity to buy and hoard what we do not need. And he is adamant that this acquisitiveness of ours can become an insurmountable barrier to genuine faith, which requires deep trust in God's providence. And "can any of you by worrying add a single hour to your span of life?" he asks. And "why do you worry about clothing? Consider the lilies of the field, how they grow; they neither toil nor spin, yet I tell you, even Solomon in all his glory was not clothed like one of these" (Matthew 6:27–29).

The temptation is to assume that Jesus is simply engaging in another of his deliberately hyperbolic ploys, perhaps to make us think but not to affect what we do. Only the supremely irresponsible person would take such a philosophy seriously. If we don't take care of ourselves, then who will?

Ancient monasticism specialized in digging out the deeper meaning of passages such as this one. And this tradition insists that Jesus is not denigrating hard work or adult responsibility but instead is taking aim at our demand for total security on our own terms. He is pointing out the underlying anxiety that compels us to store up goods we don't really need. Possessions are our hedge against the future; the more we have, the safer we will be, or at least this is how the thinking goes.

Aging brings this worry to the fore. As our eyes begin to dim, our knees to buckle, and our memory to splutter and blink out, we easily can become obsessed with security. Who will take care of us when we can no longer take care of ourselves? How will we pay for what's coming next? Employment, after all, is no longer an option. And so we cling to what we have, our purported hedge against an ominous future.

Interestingly enough, early monastic rules anticipated this intensification of anxiety in older monks. The stricture against private ownership of any kind was based on the theory that anxiety about future illness and fragility would lead to self-absorbed miserliness and thus violate the law of love. Monks would be tempted to hide gold beneath their straw pallets or bury it somewhere in the compound. Other monks would sense their preoccupation and be affected by it, possibly even being tempted into thievery. As soon as we infect others with our frantic need for security, life together becomes more competitive than cooperative. And charity becomes impossible; when we hoard resources for ourselves, we withhold them from those who might need them more than we do.

Some of my favorite monastic tales on this score come out of the Irish tradition. Early Celtic monks were an intrepid bunch, many of them sinewy ascetics who thought nothing of living on tree bark and berries or sleeping in caves. St. Brendan actually set himself adrift in the Irish Sea to prove that he had repudiated the need for worldly security and was now entirely at God's disposal. St. Columban reputedly stepped over his old mother, who was stretched out grieving across the doorsill, and spent the rest of his life on an extended pilgrimage. He trusted in his poverty to keep him focused on the task at hand, which was to establish new monastic communities throughout Europe.

Columban's blessed freedom from worry over material goods was perhaps best expressed in the *laus perennis*, the perpetual service of prayer and praise he initiated in his monasteries. No longer plagued by security issues, no longer tempted to acquire and hoard a mass of possessions meant to protect him from destitution, he lived and worked with a single-mindedness we can only dream of in this multitasking era of ours. At the end of his strange, stripped-down life, this is what he wrote to his fellow monks: "They come to tell me that the ship is ready. The end of my parchment compels me to finish my letter. Love is not orderly; it is this which has made it confused. Farewell, dear hearts of mine; pray for me that I may live in God."[15] And off he went to his cave to prepare himself for death.

My mom postponed the Forest Dweller stage as long as possible and then entered it only under duress. Like a lot of people in their mid-eighties, she had been in the same house for forty years and was perfectly content with her life, thank you very much. When one or the other of us siblings would tentatively broach the notion of downsizing, she'd give us a smug look and tell us she had "a plan," so not to trouble ourselves with her business. When I finally questioned her about that—what *is* this plan of yours, Mom?—she said it was very simple: she was going to leave that house in a six-foot box, and not before.

Then she was diagnosed with macular degeneration, and the five of us, her interfering children, met and came to a decision. It was time to push her harder than we ever had; it was time for her to stop driving. What followed was unforeseen. After a short scuffle ("I'm a good driver! What do you mean I have to stop driving?"), she gave in and began to think about what she would do next, for without the car she could not continue living alone in that house.

Shortly thereafter, she came up on the train to check out our area. We trooped through mobile home parks and condos and senior residences. We looked at the possibility of her living on our property. She kept her thoughts mostly to herself, but by the end of that week, she'd found a place she liked: a 540-square-foot apartment where transportation was provided. But there was still the problem of her house, a rambling old Spanish-style adobe filled with books, paintings, music, diaries, photos, computer equipment, a grand piano, and a plethora of mementoes from her many travels.

Once again, the clan of siblings gathered. We rented a full-sized dumpster for the driveway. We bought stacks of cardboard boxing material. And then we dug in.

Two days into the process, I straightened up, pushed back my sweaty hair, and took a good hard look at my mom. We were working on her room by now, the one with the most bookcases and biggest files, the room she'd shared with my dad until his early death twenty years before. This one room alone housed a lifetime of accumulated memories. The work was laborious; nobody wanted to accidentally throw away or give away something she was going to miss. So there she sat in a straight-backed chair, boxes piled around her, hour after hour making spur-of-the-moment decisions about what to do with items she'd saved, in some cases, for decades. By the time it hit me just how hard this must be for her—how brave she was being—we'd already put her through two ten-hour days of it. We were focused on the task; what was *she* focused on? What was going through her mind?

I never found out; when it came down to it, I could not bear to ask. Unlike me, the penultimate shedder of possessions, my mom had devoted herself to the preservation of artifacts. And some of these were astonishing. We found my mother's wedding dress. We found our elementary-school report cards. We found homemade birthday cards and receipts for furniture purchased in the early sixties and recipes from my long-dead grandmothers. And then my sister Gail opened a shoe box stashed high on the closet shelf and pulled out a stack of five lined notebooks, one for each of us, in which our mother had recorded in meticulous detail our first months on earth. When I opened my own, I found an envelope inside containing a lock of golden hair.

This was mine? My very own nearly sixty-year-old baby hair? I touched it with one finger, lightly, as though it might crumble like something from an Egyptian tomb. This hair had grown upon my infant head. And my mother had taken the time to clip this little spray, curl it into a fragile spiral, and put it away for the moment that had just arrived.

I set it down carefully and slipped out of the room for a brief, tearful snuffle. This was the antithesis of monastic simplicity, this loving storing up of family mementoes. And until this moment, I had never appreciated my mother's ways. In fact, I had felt a mite superior in that regard—me, the off-loader of my children's blue cockatiel and their ancient fish. Who was right? Which was better—affectionate clutter or serene spareness?

I cannot answer that question for anyone but myself. What I do know is that once that wrenching five days ended, once we had packed up the few possessions and pieces of furniture that would fit in her new place, my mom, nervous as she was about starting all over without the cherished mementoes of a lifetime to give her courage, seemed to straighten up, throw back her shoulders, and shyly but eagerly test the air.

4
Settling

*You see that my dwelling is destitute of water; but I pray you,
let us beseech him who turned solid rock into water and stones
into fountains that . . . he may vouchsafe to open to us a
spring of water, even from this stony rock.*[16]
—*Cuthbert (c. 635–687)*

Twenty-five years after moving onto our land, I noticed something
interesting. Certain kinds of plants came up on their own, then grew
and spread without any help from me. Naturally, I knew that weeds
did this; I'd been locked in a death battle with weeds for years. These
were different. For one thing, they were shrubs, sometimes herba-
ceous, sometimes woody. For another, they did not come up in my
garden, like those greedy weeds, but in the pine forest or among the
native oaks—solitary seedlings with only two small leaves at first,
but obviously incredibly tenacious. By the time I gave them my first
real look, some of them had branched out, become treelike, and
started small nurslings in the surrounding oak duff.

Were they beautiful? Not really, not at first. I was used to buying
plants at the local nursery, a damp, humus-y, jungle-like place with
no environmental similarity to our land. I chose my plants solely
on the basis of their looks, dutifully reading their labels to find out
whether they needed full sun or shade, lots of water or little. And
I made my choices while lost in a happy vision of how spectacular
they would be in the spot I'd already picked out for them, regardless

of their actual needs. When they survived, I considered it a miracle—and it was.

Now, however, I found myself increasingly interested in these plain-Jane interlopers who were slowly populating our four acres, because it was clear they'd been at this undetected colonization for several decades by now. I wondered who they were and how they did so well without a bit of care from me. One day I found out.

Our friend Bill dropped by, casually mentioning on his way out the door that we had some nice toyon growing down below the barn. "Toyon?" I asked. "What's toyon?"

"You know. Dark green? Red berries? What they named the city of Hollywood after? The birds love it when it starts to fruit."

"But where did it come from? I didn't plant it."

He gave me a pitying look. "It's a California native. You've got lots of natives growing on this place: Prunus ilicifolia. Rhamnus californica. Artemisia."

"No kidding!" This was amazing. Not a dollar spent at the nursery, and here were all these flourishing plants. "Will you show me which is which?"

"I'll do better than that," he said. "I'll loan you my library."

And so it was that I took up a short but intense botanical study, wowed on a daily basis by what I had missed all these years. The area in which we live, the California Central Coast, is considered to be one of the most ideal climates in the world. Only four other areas can compare: the western part of the Cape of South Africa, Central Coastal Chile, the Mediterranean coastline, and the southwestern corner of Australia. Our particular native species can survive in those places, and theirs can happily migrate to ours. But what, I thought, was the need? We were blessed with a plethora of plants all our own, uniquely adapted to the particular soils of our coast, to the winds, the winter chill, the summer highs, and most of all, the limited, precious winter rains. These plants could grow by themselves, without any help from me, because for eons they'd been developing in concert with their environmental conditions.

This was absolutely grand, and I decided that the least I could do was help out the immigrant toyon. After all, our land had been stripped of everything except the coastal oaks nearly sixty years before; who knew what wonderful natives had been destroyed in the process? It was only right for me to do what I could for the cause. But what to plant? In one of Bill's books I came across a picture of a shrub I'd always admired but had never been able to identify before. It was a ten-footer with forest green leaves and, every spring, copper-yellow flowers the size of my fist. This fremontia would look *fantastic* right below the house where everyone could see the blossom show. Never mind that it was just a mite shady in that spot.

I found a nursery that carried my plant, paid extra for the five-gallon version, and dug a hole bigger than required so that I could add the amendments that Bill's book specifically said it did not need and would not like. But a little fertilizer couldn't hurt, could it? It would grow faster, which could only be good. Then I put it on an every-three-day watering schedule, despite the nursery guy's warning that fremontias, a.k.a. flannel bushes, were extremely skittish about wet feet. Every so often I gave it an extra gulp when it looked a little peaked—which mysteriously began happening within a week or two of its arrival on our property.

What to do? I called the nursery guy, who asked, with some suspicion, how much I was watering it. "Not all that much," I prevaricated. "It's been pretty hot, you know."

"Seventy-two is hot?"

"Well . . ."

"My guess is that you're overwatering."

This was suddenly my guess, too. Filled with an upsurge of guilt, I rushed to the side of my failing fremontia and detached the drip line, pouring a gallon of diluted B-1 into the basin, just in case it was suffering from shock. Two days later, leaves began to fall. Within another week, the plant was bare, and the growing tips had turned black. I called the nursery guy again. There was a long silence. "Any theories?" he finally asked. Clearly, he'd decided that my flannel bush was in a terminal decline, and, even more clearly, that this was nobody's fault but my own.

~~~~~

I am sitting on a bench in the Hermitage cloister with my friend Janet, whose tranquil loveliness belies her legendary courage. The October air is chilly, but the sun in this protected garden is warm. Janet has her eyes closed and her face turned to the sky. Her cane is propped against the bench, and I can just make out beneath her jeans the outline of her leg brace, an ingenious piece of equipment that lets her administer small shocks to her bad leg when she needs some extra *oomph* to keep her going. She's a year younger than I am, and she was diagnosed with multiple sclerosis shortly after she turned fifty-three.

We have been friends for nearly twenty-five years. Janet introduced me to the Catholic Church. It was she who brought me to the Hermitage for the first time. Six years later, we made our oblate vows together, with our spouses and kids in the congregation. In the early days of our friendship, we spent a lot of time walking or hiking. Like me, Janet was an avid backpacker, but unlike me, she was also an accomplished horsewoman. On one memorable occasion, she was run by a skittish horse into the horizontal bough of a coastal live oak tree. Dazed, she picked herself off the ground, caught the horse, got back in the saddle, rode home, and proceeded to cook dinner for a group of friends. Then she went to bed and, in the middle of the night, woke her husband and said she might need to go to the hospital. Turned out, she'd broken a number of ribs and collapsed a lung. But this was Janet, a woman whose irresistibly serene face you would not be surprised to see in a seventeenth-century Dutch masterpiece.

I wonder how her inherent toughness has or has not helped her adjust to a precipitous physical decline that, unlike those broken ribs, will only get worse. I wonder whether it has helped her deal with the early onset of aging, because that is what she is now—old well before her time. She is gradually losing her balance and often falls. Her leg works only on a part-time basis. She suffers almost constant pain. And she has, by her own estimate, only about half of her usual energy, which must be guarded carefully each day if she's going to make it all the way through to evening. I wonder how these unexpected circumstances have affected her relationship with God—she is a person of deep faith. So I ask.

Janet is quiet, her eyes still closed against the sun. I hope I haven't offended her.

"I got pretty angry with him for a while. I couldn't understand what he was doing, why he was letting this happen to me."

"I can imagine."

She sighs. "It took a while—maybe six months?—but finally I got sick of being mad. Then I didn't know what to do. I wasn't ready to accept this yet, but I couldn't go on blaming God either. I just felt lost and sad."

A couple of monks pass through the cloister on their way to the bookstore, and both of us nod and smile. Though guests are normally not invited to this part of the monastery, we are legitimate. We have a date with the ailing Fr. Bernard, and someone has gone to fetch him from his cell.

"How did you handle it?" I ask.

"I started swimming. Every few days. And I found that I could do things with my body in the water that I couldn't do on land anymore—like flutter kick with my bad leg. And when I was doing my laps, just staring down at the bottom of the pool, I started saying the rosary—'Hail, Mary, full of grace,' reach, kick, reach, kick—and that felt good, too. So things started slowly getting better."

"You mean physically?"

"Not outside the water. But I felt more peace about everything. I decided that God must still have something for me to do in life, even if I don't know what it is yet."

"You found a purpose again."

"I found peace. That's the only way I can put it."

Then both of us hear a familiar shuffle. Fr. Bernard is making his tortoise-like way in our direction, and the discussion is over. I would like to ask her more. I'd like to know how a person moves from that level of anger and disappointment and no doubt fearfulness about the future to what she calls "peace." But it seems unfair to push her, a person who does not talk much as it is. So instead, I hang on to the image of her swimming and praying in the wavery green light of the pool.

Ancient monasticism developed between two seemingly opposite poles: pilgrimage and settling. Monks like Columban spent their lives in imitation of their peripatetic master, Jesus, who voluntarily gave up a place to lay his head. Life on the road ensured they would not get overly attached to any one place; the necessity of carrying everything on their backs took care of any temptations toward avarice. Pilgrims were in a very real way the freest of free beings, and their lives were inherently adventurous, for they were constantly moving forward into mystery.

Yet equally important was the monastic injunction to never leave one's cell. "Sit in your cell as in a paradise," begins the Brief Rule of the tenth-century St. Romuald of Ravenna, founder of the Camaldolese. This bit of wisdom comes straight from the much-earlier desert mothers and fathers, who ranged far into the Egyptian, Palestinian, and Syrian wilderness in search of solitude, silence, and prayer. Also, "Your cell will teach you everything." If only the monks could bear the at-times crushing boredom of their own four walls, not to mention the resultant urge to flee, they might well be made holy in the fiery crucible of stasis. The men and women who took this route often became solitaries and hermits.

One man, the seventh-century St. Cuthbert, spent a good deal of time on the road before taking up the eremitical lifestyle for which he is best known. In his early days as prior of Melrose on the River Tweed in the Scottish borderlands, he could not bear the thought that whenever trouble struck, local believers resorted to their old pagan ways. So despite his duties at the monastery, he regularly traveled to the surrounding villages, earnestly teaching his vulnerable flock about life in Christ. Wherever he preached, people were drawn by his gentle, obviously loving concern for their spiritual well-being.

Yet in the midst of this important apostolic work, Cuthbert increasingly longed for contemplative silence and solitude. After being transferred to the island of Lindisfarne to oversee the monastery there, he asked for and received permission to become a recluse on the islet of Farne, which, as his biographer, the Venerable Bede, so quaintly put it, lies small and insignificant on the surface of "the Ocean."[17] Cuthbert built earthen ramparts around it to hold back the tides and spent his days praying and attending to his barley crop, the only thing that would grow in the barren, sandy soil. At night he gazed up at an ocean of stars. Like other hermits before him, however, the longer he maintained his contemplative solitude, the greater his reputation for holiness grew. After ten years of increasing pressure to return to public life, he reluctantly left his cell in the sea to take up an administrative post as bishop of Lindisfarne.

Yet Cuthbert continued to yearn for the silence of Farne. Sensing that he was about to die, he resigned his post and returned to his beloved islet, where he succumbed to a fatal illness within months. He was buried the same day at the Lindisfarne monastery. Twelve years later when, by custom, the monks dug up his bones in order to clean them, they discovered to their amazement that his body had not yet decayed. In fact, he looked like a man asleep, a sure sign of saintliness. His coffin was placed inside the church, and pilgrims began coming to Lindisfarne to be healed. It was generally believed that the island was blessed because of Cuthbert's incorrupt presence.

Two centuries later, however, the first Viking raids out of Denmark began, and the monks of the island decided they must flee, carrying the precious body of Cuthbert with them. Thus, the man who most longed to "sit in his cell as in a paradise" began a several-centuries-long road trip. Transported on the shoulders of his intrepid caretakers, he was hidden in first one place, then anoth, sometimes for years at a time, while the terrifying northmen repeat-edly struck at the coastlines of Scotland and England. Eventually, he wound up at Durham, where he stayed put for nearly a hundred years before the looming threat posed by William the Conquerer convinced his loyal retainers they must once again spirit his remains to safety. So back he went to Lindisfarne for a brief time. It was not until the twelfth century that he found his final resting place, once again at Durham.

Cuthbert had finally settled.

To "settle" in the spiritual sense means to stop questing. To settle is to put down roots in whatever soil lies beneath us, no matter how arid or rocky, no matter how seemingly bereft.

Yet if there is any philosophy that flies in the face of con-temporary wisdom, it is this notion of settling down. We are an inherently restless people. We are striving for so many important things, after all: self-esteem, self-reliance, self-fulfillment. Our cul-tural stake in individualism demands that we continue this personal quest, no matter how tired we might be. And the older we get, the more urgent the mission to achieve what we most want out of our ephemeral existence. This is it, we think—even those of us who ostensibly believe in the promise of eternal life. Our time on this earth seems so achingly brief that we feel we cannot afford to waste a moment doing what looks like nothing. Yet one of the deepest insights gained by those monastics of the desert is that we must end this quest and finally settle down if we are ever to find real wisdom.

What can the attempt to settle teach us? First, that we are restless creatures, always on the lookout for stimulation wherever we might find it. Without extensive training and discipline, we can focus only for relatively brief periods, no matter how we try. Buddhists run

into this disconcerting fact over and over again when they attempt
to meditate and meet the "monkey mind" instead. And like the
desert fathers, they reach for the same antidote: sit still, and hope for
the best.

The attempt to settle also forces us to confront a difficult question about meaning. Questing, after all, sends us after what is finer
and higher and more satisfying, so how can we give it up? When
we quest, we cannot help but feel larger than ourselves, even noble.
We are *seeking*. We are striving. We are aiming far above the merely
pragmatic; our sights are set on the transcendent. Doesn't St. Aelred
of Rievaulx talk about our built-in longing for the "homeland of our
hope," a place that lies at the edges of our capacity for understanding?[18] Doesn't questing sit at the very heart of religion itself?

The answer is yes, but with some qualifications. It is perfectly
possible to make a mistake about what is ultimate in life, to set our
sights on an illusory goal. We can also get mixed up about why
we are doing what we are doing, even (or maybe, especially) when
our quest is all wrapped up in religious aspirations. Even a legitimate spiritual quest can become all-consuming, and we ourselves
can become so future-oriented that we lose touch with the actual circumstances of our lives. We begin to live in a feverish dream, our
eyes fixed on a distant and ever-receding horizon. We fail to see that
our quotidian existence—the simple exigencies of natural life—have
much to teach us about our spiritual purpose.

What's more important to understand is that in our endless
questing, we never stumble on a beautiful secret: that God's
time—*kairos* time—is always present and available to us, even in
the daily dawnings and dyings of the circadian cycle. At any instant,
if only we are aware enough to catch it, we can enter a suspended
moment that contains within it layer upon layer of history, the

multiple petals of the present, and the swirling mists of the future to come.

In the right spirit, it is possible to enter *kairos* time no matter what the circumstances. But it certainly becomes easier when the taste for stimulating distractions and the energy for questing have dissipated on their own, which happens naturally during aging or because of untimely illness, as in Janet's case. She, buoyed up by water and immersed in prayer, now regularly abides in the realm of *kairos*.

The untimely death of my fremontia plant had its effect on me. It was one thing to lose exotic plants to an unwelcoming environment—an expensive mistake, but understandable. To lose a California native, planted in the soil it was designed to occupy, meant there was something askew in the gardener herself. Chastened, I went back to Bill's books, this time paying attention to facts I'd blithely set aside before. Flannel bushes, it seems, do not appreciate meddling, no matter how well-meant. They are natural solitaries that, once they take root and settle in, grow slowly for the first few years, testing themselves against the sand and the rocks, the wind and the gophers, and most of all, the endless months of complete aridity.

If they survive the testing—and left alone, most of them do—they will begin to flourish and grow until, in less than a decade, they might reach ten feet tall. And given adequate winter rain, every spring they will burst into light: a thousand copper-yellow suns among the dark green leaves.

This was something worth waiting for. I planted four more flannel bushes, babies this time. Once I had them settled in their sandy little holes, I covered my eyes and tiptoed away, consigning them to the hands of their Maker.

5
Confronting

*And when the Evil One brandishes his sword against you, you
break it in his own heart.*[19]
—*Hildegarde of Bingen (1098–1179)*

I was a thirty-two-year-old single mom, a would-be writer without
a college degree, struggling hard to make ends meet. Andrea was
in first grade, Johnny in kindergarten, and after getting the two of
them off to school in the morning, I drove to my morning job as a
clerk at the local community college. At lunchtime, I headed for my
other job, another half-time clerical position at the university library
six miles away. By the time the workday was over, the kids picked
up from daycare, dinner made, and baths and stories over, it was
usually 10 p.m. or later. That was the only time I had to write, so
that's when I did it—sitting with a glass of wine at a rickety linoleum
kitchen table in a dilapidated mountainside cabin, the only single
family dwelling I could afford to rent. I'd convinced myself, and
done my best to convince the kids, that it would be *rustic*, that we
would love it there; but that was before we moved in. Haunted and
mice-ridden, the cabin gave all three of us the willies.

Money was tighter than tight. But one day I got a phone call
from a friend who taught film at the university. He'd been contacted
by a local man who was willing to pay a ghostwriter up to $10,000
to craft the tale of his fascinating life. My friend thought of me, who
could only gape in awe at the thought of all that cash. Would I be

interested? I laughed out loud. There was one glitch, my friend hastened to add: though he'd been out of prison for years by now, the guy had spent over three decades there. This gave me pause, but not for long. Soon I had embarked on one of the more foolish enterprises of my life.

Frank, age eighty, turned out to be my height—five-foot-five-inches—but with disturbingly over-developed biceps for his age. He also had the abundant hair, flat face, and fixed stare of a KGB agent. Though he was impressed that I, a woman, would drink beer from a can (a test he ran on me during our first meeting), he also made it clear from the start who was boss. The book itself was secondary to his real aim, which was to see his life portrayed on the big screen. He'd already chosen the star who would play him. All I had to do was write a best seller that would get the attention of Hollywood. And despite having hired me at a fairly significant rate of pay to take the job out of his unqualified hands, he fully planned to oversee every step of the creative process.

This momentarily took me aback. I was a young, idealistic writer, still unpublished, which meant I was unused to having anyone interfere with my work. But no matter, because I was out of my mind with excitement. Multiple murder convictions! One of the longest running prison terms in U.S. history! His partner executed in the chair! Not to mention trunk loads of news clippings, letters from immigrant relatives, and *True Crime* magazine articles detailing his exploits. Truly a writer's dream story.

Yet in the midst of my anticipatory glee, I was also aware of a growing apprehension. I talked with my film professor friend, who confessed to more than a little nervousness on my behalf. I *was* a single mother; I *did* live alone in a shaky old mountainside cabin. What was to stop this volatile ex-con from terrorizing me? Worse, what if something went wrong with the deal?

We decided I should not take the money up front, much as I needed it. Instead, I'd write the book, and whatever I sold it for, Frank and I would split down the middle. Frank was suspicious at first—what woman in her right mind would turn down an easy ten grand? But eventually he reconciled himself to a collaborative relationship rather than the dictatorship he much preferred, and we got down to business.

Every time Johnny and Andrea were with their dad, I was with Frank, taping hours of interviews. He talked about his immigrant childhood in Minneapolis, the nefarious mentor who lured him into a life of crime before he was fifteen, the bank robberies and getaways, and the murders he insisted were not his fault. The longer I listened, the more I began to wonder whether Frank had even begun to confront the truth about his past or if he was instead wedded to a self-deceptive fantasy about who he was and why his life had unfolded the way it had. Was I devoting a huge chunk of my precious time and creative energy to someone who was still, in his ninth decade, living a lie?

Everything came to a head eighteen months later when Mike, my fiancé, and I flew to Minneapolis so that I could interview Frank's relatives. We were due to be married soon, and this seemed like the best way to start wrapping up the all-absorbing book project so that we could get on with our new life. However, the Minneapolis clan, presumably the people who knew Frank best and loved him most, only confirmed my suspicions. One of them asked in obvious exasperation, "Why would anyone want to read about a guy like *him*?" Nobody in the family bought his self-serving rendition of the facts, and several of his relatives bluntly warned me that he was still a tough and untrustworthy customer and that I should be careful.

Frank himself, who with his long-suffering wife had followed us to Minneapolis in his ancient blue van, grew increasingly agitated the longer we stuck around. Though at first he'd been excited to show us his old digs—the original family home, the scene of his first robbery, his favorite hideout—now he was snappish and irritable whenever I suggested another possible pilgrim site. Then the blue van began to splutter, and when the guy at the mechanic shop told him it would be a couple of days before they could fix it, Frank blew. Grabbing a tire iron off the shelf, he brandished it at the mechanic, demanding they get to work immediately. Mike took me by the arm and pulled me into the adjoining garage. "Listen," he said, "you've got to get out of this. I don't care how much time you've got invested. This is crazy." I had nothing to say; all I could do was nod mutely. It was clear to both of us that Frank was indeed capable of the murders he insisted weren't his fault. And for the past year and a half, I'd been helping him construct the narrative he hoped would finally exonerate him in the eyes of the world.

I did not dare confront him right then. As soon as we were safely home, I wrote Frank a letter telling him the deal was off. And just as my professor friend had predicted, Frank did not take it well. I'd strung him along, he said, and I would pay for it. Before Frank could make it back to our town to carry out his threats, however, Mike and I had gotten married and moved the kids into a new house, making sure our address and phone number were unlisted. Frank had no way to find us. Yet I did not sleep well again until I heard from one of the Minneapolis relatives about his death a few years later. As far as anybody could tell, he remained unrepentant to the end, leaving this world without ever confronting his past or seeking absolution for his many sins.

~~~~~~

In Jesus' day, the wilderness was thought to be the abode of Satan and his minions. Three hundred years later, nothing had changed; people went to the desert expecting to confront evil. Thus, when a person gave up his life in the world for silence, solitude, and prayer, he was also signing up for a harrowing spiritual adventure. The first of the great Christian hermits, St. Anthony the Great, frequently engaged in exhausting physical combat with the devil. The monks who followed in his footsteps maintained freezing all-night vigils in order to pray for the protection of sleeping and vulnerable people everywhere. For centuries to come, monks would see themselves as spiritual warriors, and many of the great saints until modern times spoke of personal run-ins with malevolent spirits.

Yet even in the days when Satan's interfering presence in a believer's life was unquestioned, evil was never located entirely outside the self. One's private thoughts—lustful thoughts, envious thoughts, vengeful thoughts, self-pitying thoughts—could unbar the door to the soul, rendering one defenseless against attack by opportunistic spiritual forces. The fourth-century monk, Evagrius Ponticus, wrote about eight particularly dangerous thoughts, or *logismoi*. Besides lust, anger, and self-pitying sadness, these included gluttony, acedia (a spirit of futility regarding spiritual practice), avarice (greed), vainglory (the hunger for public acclaim and praise), and cold-hearted pride. These *logismoi* in and of themselves were not sinful, but they were compelling, and too often, a person could not help himself. He would begin to interact with these thoughts, to cherish them, and finally to identify himself with them. At this point, he was now in bondage and could not get free on his own.

Evagrius's Eight Evil Thoughts inspired antidotal spiritual practices. Those who suffered from gluttony were advised to fast. Those who were obsessed by their possessions were advised to give all they had to the poor. Those who lusted were advised to practice chastity. The point of these ascetical practices was to trigger self-recognition and eventually, true self-knowledge and humility. The practical goal was freedom from the countless distractions spawned by mindless self-pleasing. The mystical goal was purity of heart, or transformation into a more Christlike being. Yet none of this could begin without a willingness to confront evil, both in the self and in the world. The biggest impediment to this process was living in a state of denial.

By the time one of my heroes, the medieval saint Hildegarde of Bingen, was born in 1098, the Eight Evil Thoughts had become the Seven Deadly Sins. The once-clear connection between thought patterns and sin patterns had given way to a more juridical understanding of moral wrongdoing. Instead of highlighting our psychological vulnerability to temptation, as Evagrius and the monastic desert tradition had done, the Seven Deadlies focused on acts for which we needed to make formal confession and receive absolution. Yet some people, including Hildegarde, still understood the ancient view with its focus on mental processes. Her interest in the mind led her to write a book of diagnoses for psychological disorders and suggestions for homeopathic cures. She was also reputed to be a wise counselor, or soul doctor.

Hildegarde's spiritual training came through a series of visions that began when she was quite young. As she puts it, "From my infancy until now . . . my soul has always beheld [the] Light; and in it my soul soars to the summit of the firmament and into a different air. . . . Sometimes when I see it, all sadness and pain is lifted from me, and I seem a simple girl again, and an old woman no more."[20] Her mentor was Jutta, an anchoress, or solitary, to whom she was given as a child.

What was the fruit of this visionary existence? As in the days of the desert dwellers, along with a clarification of spiritual vision came the ability to recognize and confront evil when she saw it. Thus, from middle age on, St. Hildegarde dedicated herself to reforming her beloved but increasingly corrupt church. Much like St. Catherine of Siena several hundred years later, Hildegarde was no respecter of persons. Her letters to lackadaisical priests, ambitious bishops, self-indulgent cardinals, tyrannical kings, and erring popes are astonishing in their bluntness, given the position of women in her day. Yet despite the radical role she played, she had no desire to change the structure of the church or any of its doctrines; she saw herself instead as a prophetic voice, calling men back to their true vocations in a time of spiritual crisis.

Such a straightforward attitude toward evil seems, in our time, archaic if not actually dangerous. We believe that we have grown beyond making such clear-cut distinctions between good and evil. We try our best to accept the differences—including the differences in moral attitudes—between one another. We believe that in a pluralistic society, this is the way to peace. New Age thought draws deeply from this well, suggesting that our habit of passing judgment, even on ourselves, is an obstacle to genuine enlightenment. Wisdom is achieved when we realize that we are perfect as we are.

Yet this is not the philosophical ground on which Jesus walked. He spoke often of evil and did not hesitate to point it out. For example, he criticized the hypocrisy of the Pharisees who required the people to do what they themselves only preached but didn't practice. He dramatically overturned the money changers' tables in the temple. Before he even began his ministry, he engaged in a forty-day struggle with Satan in the wilderness. When he healed people, he often told them to "go and sin no more" (John 8:11). And a large percentage of these healings were actually exorcisms.

How do we reconcile the gospel view of evil with the contemporary sensibilities that urge us toward moral tolerance? The key is the same as it was in Jesus' time or in the time of the desert dwellers or in Hildegarde's day: *love*. All moral judgment must be driven by love or it will itself become evil. As St. Paul says, "Love is patient; love is kind; love is not envious or boastful or arrogant or rude. It does not insist on its own way; it is not irritable or resentful; it does not rejoice in wrongdoing, but rejoices in the truth. It bears all things, believes all things, hopes all things, endures all things" (1 Corinthians 13:4–7).

And the rule of love applies to self-judgment also. We are called to genuine self-knowledge, which means that in the interest of truth, we are called to drop the self-protective barriers of denial. But we are never called to hate ourselves or to live in a state of permanent shame or unshakeable guilt or endless regret. As it says in 1 Corinthians 13, love may be the greatest of the three theological virtues, but faith and hope are just as important in the life of the spirit; all three are denied when we fall into an abyss of despair over our sins.

Aging presents us with the opportunity, perhaps our final opportunity, for confronting the evil in ourselves and in the people we most love. When we let the moment slip past, terrified at what we might discover, we remain in a spiritually crippling state of denial. We also miss a great opportunity to speak a healing word of truth to someone who might never otherwise receive it.

One of the saddest interviews I taped during my year and a half with Frank was with his wife, Sylvia. She was a gentle woman who, before Frank burst into her life, had long since given up on the dream of marriage, devoting herself instead to caring for her aged parents. One of her few pleasures was going to an occasional dance at the local recreation center. A few days after Frank was finally released from the penitentiary, he showed up at the same center. With a cheap bouquet hidden behind his back, he scanned the floor with his KGB stare. He knew exactly who he was looking for: a middle-aged spinster who might be amenable to his charms despite his astonishingly lengthy prison record. As he cynically boasted to me, he was looking for a woman who was "desperate," and he chose well; before the end of the evening, he'd talked her into going to a motel room with him, her first-ever experience of what she shyly characterized as "love" in her interview with me.

Sylvia's need for Frank to be the prince charming she'd waited so long to meet carried her through the ensuing years, despite his raging temper and self-deceptive lies. She never told me what those years were like; based on my own experience of his incorrigible egoism, however, I'm sure they were hell. Yet she was so deeply invested in the relationship that she willed herself into blindness—not the blindness of humble, genuine love, in which every judgment regarding another becomes implicitly a judgment against ourselves—but instead the blindness of desperation. And when I broke off the relationship with Frank, she, who of all people should have known exactly why, rushed angrily to his defense.

Instead, she might have been his guide, the partner who loved him enough to help him confront and perhaps even vanquish the demons who controlled his life. She might have helped him relinquish his grandiose quest to rewrite his shameful history. She might have helped him face death with a clear conscience.

As, perhaps, I might have done, if I'd had any relationship with God back then. If I'd been less focused on my own ambitions. If I'd been older, wiser, and past my own years of willful self-deception.

I might even have been Frank's Hildegarde.

6
Accepting

*Our Lord gave me a spiritual insight into the unpretentious
manner of his loving. I saw that for us he is everything that is
good, comforting and helpful; he is our clothing, who, for love,
wraps us up, holds us close; he entirely encloses us for tender
love, so that he may never leave us, since he is the source of all
good things for us.*[21]
—*Julian of Norwich (c. 1343–1417)*

Both Mike and I come by our love of the land honestly—in his
case, via his Scotch-Irish farmer forebears and in mine, through
great-great grandparents who left their tenancies in Norway during
the middle of the nineteenth century to homestead the Minnesota
plains. My father was born and raised on the family farm, and I
could have grown up there, too. Instead, we went west, and my dad's
twin brother, Lowell, a Norwegian bachelor farmer of the first ilk,
stayed and kept it going. One of his proudest moments came when
he received an award for 150 years of continual farming by the same
family on the same land.

Though my dad moved us to California when I was two, every
few years he sacrificed his vacation to drive his ever-growing brood
back to the farm. In this midwestern Eden, we gangly kids from the
L.A. suburbs picked strawberries, potatoes, and green beans from my
grandmother's loamy garden. We eased eggs from beneath slit-eyed
hens. We shelled peas, candled eggs, cracked walnuts, and cranked

ice cream. From the time I was old enough to think, I could not imagine any better way to live. The farm was my anchor and my source, my wellspring of delight. It also provided me with a vision of beauty, order, and simplicity that I later found reflected in monastic life.

The family homestead was so essential to my worldview that it was only after I had become a young adult and my competent grandma had transitioned into a ninety-two-year-old Alzheimer's patient in a skilled nursing center that the thought finally occurred to me: What will become of the farm when Uncle Lowell gets old? But this question was too upsetting to contemplate, so I shoved it aside and did not allow myself to think of it again until many years later, when the issue was finally forced upon us.

⁓⌇⌇⌐

Two of my favorite bits of monastic wisdom come from Fr. Bernard. Years ago, a big-city newspaper contacted the Hermitage for permission to do a feature story. The pretty young reporter assigned to the job brought a photographer with her, who spent the day trying to herd the monks into spontaneous-looking groups. They were not, according to Fr. Bernard, very cooperative. He, on the other hand, having the heart of a Frenchman, was highly simpatico with women, and he felt sorry for this young lady, who'd clearly never waded into such deep water before. So he stuck around to see if he could help.

This meant he wound up being interviewed at length—a scene that, knowing Fr. Bernard as well as I did, was hard to imagine. How had she kept him on topic? How many jokes had he trotted out? How had she navigated that tricky French-Canadian accent, no doubt intensified by the romantic thrill of being in her attractive young presence? When he proudly handed me a copy of the newspaper the next time I visited, I made as if to put it away for later, not wanting to risk blanching in front of him. But he insisted that I read it then and there.

Fr. Bernard, I found, had PR skills I'd never suspected. Not only had he conducted himself with statesmanlike dignity, but also he'd summed up in a single sentence the whole point of the monastic enterprise. Why did you become a monk? the reporter had asked him. Because life is short, he replied calmly, and I wanted to live it the best way I could.

On another occasion, a first-time visitor asked Fr. Bernard how he managed to keep his eyes on God through all his decades at the Hermitage. Don't you ever get sick of this? Don't you sometimes wish you were doing something else? Fr. Bernard shook his head, pointing out that monks have a saying that helps keep them focused.

"What's that?" asked the visitor.

"*Memento mori*," said Fr. Bernard.

"And what does it mean?"

Fr. Bernard gave her an impish grin. "Hello, I'm going to die."

From its beginnings in the third-century Egyptian desert, Christian monasticism has concerned itself with final things. Certain stringent practitioners sometimes occupied caves used to house the dead or even slept inside their own coffins as a visceral reminder that time here on earth is limited. Physical existence, they believed, is meant to prepare us for eternal life with God. And there is no other way to meet our future except to undergo the terrible transition of death. Even people of great faith quail in the face of what, from this side of the passageway, cannot help but feel like total extinction.

Perhaps this is one of the reasons we work so hard. Hyper-productivity is a way to harden ourselves against emotional turmoil, including the stormy anguish of grief or the shocking recognition that death is imminent. We've got too much to do; we cannot afford to spend serious time in thought. Hence, one of aging's greatest challenges makes its appearance when we find ourselves too old to be productive anymore. Suddenly, we are faced with certain facts about life that we've been able to hold at bay for decades simply by keeping ourselves so busy we've had no free moments in which to ponder them.

And thus does aging increase our levels of anxiety and fearfulness. Not only do we now have hours to cogitate—an activity guaranteed to make us hardworking Americans extremely nervous—but also we're steadily losing ground in the sensory department. We hear and see less than we used to. We fumble with our fingers and trip on our own feet. We forget what we heard or read two minutes ago. We're constantly falling asleep in the big blue chair. Some of us, medicated for various medical conditions, begin to experience vivid hallucinations that make it extremely difficult to sort out what is real and what is not. When we're constantly losing important items (the keys, the checkbook, the wallet), it's easier to blame others than to face the facts. The combination of frustration and suspicion can lead to elaborate conspiracy theories. No surprise, then, that senior paranoia is widespread; reality and the looming specter of death are simply too painful to bear.

Monastic *memento mori* disrupts this vicious cycle. A daily meditation on dying can ease death's threatening sting, and it can also help us bear the grief that accompanies loss. The practice of *memento mori* reminds us that everything—our fondest memories of childhood, the physical relics of our most joyful moments, our very ability to see, hear, walk, and remember—are passing away, too. We cannot hold on to a single thing, no matter how we try. For this is the way of all flesh; naked we arrive and naked shall we depart. Many of the ascetical practices of monasticism are undergirded by *memento mori*. Disciplines such as fasting, celibacy, silence, and solitude highlight the ephemeral nature of the physical realm and thus force us to confront the brevity of earthly existence.

What are some practical steps we can take to keep the reality of death before our eyes, especially in a society that tries its best to avoid the subject completely? First, every time we look into the mirror, we can gently remind ourselves that this person we have come to know so well is in the process of dying, and has been ever since birth. Nobody escapes; everyone is on the same road, including the youngest and freshest among us. Like birth, death is an experience that we all share, so why do we fear it so?

Second, when we catch ourselves making long-term plans—in five years I will be doing this, in ten, this—we can stop and pray these words: God willing. During past eras when death took so many children and young adults, people tended to make fewer assumptions about the future and to more consciously place the future in God's hands.

Finally, we can "keep our bags packed," in the sense that we are always prepared to make the journey out of this earthly existence, no matter when that journey begins. And one extremely important preparation for death is to have our affairs in order. Is there somebody we still need to forgive? Is there a relationship that needs healing? Is there something we are guilty about but have never confessed? To practice *memento mori* means to take care of these obligations while we still can.

Though the remembrance of death has always been important in monasticsm, it particularly characterizes the lifestyle called *anchoritism*. The anchorites came into their own during medieval times and are strongly associated with England, where many archaeological remains of their anchorholds still remain. English anchorites usually lived in small cells attached to the sides of churches. Their entry into the anchorhold was permanent, and many of them were actually walled in. From the tenth century on, passage into the anchoritic life was marked by a funeral-like procession culminating with the bishop's saying from the Office of the Dead: "From dust you were created, to dust you shall return." In all important respects, the anchorite had died to the world.

Most cells had three windows. A hagioscope, or "squint," allowed the anchoress (for they were often women) to participate in the Mass and to receive communion. A second aperture allowed her to communicate with a servant, who supplied her daily needs. Another small opening on the outer wall of the cell allowed her to counsel the people who came seeking her advice as her reputation for holiness grew. For in addition to her greatest duty as an anchorite—to pray for the dead in purgatory—she was also meant to be a soul doctor. Unlike "normal" people, she spoke as one who had already made the long journey from life through death and onward into the realm of mystery.

Probably the greatest of the English anchorites, and certainly the most famous, is Julian of Norwich. At the age of thirty she received a series of visions, or "showings," as she called them, over a period of many hours. She meditated on these visions for years. The book in which she finally recorded them, *A Revelation of Love*, became the first book written in English by a woman. She begins with these words: "These revelations were shown to a simple unlettered creature, the year of our Lord 1373, the 13th day of May."[22]

When she was about fifty years old, she moved into a small cell attached to St. Julian's Church, where she would live out the rest of her life, praying for those layfolk she always referred to as her "even Christians."[23] Beyond anything else, she wanted them to experience the love of God in the way she herself had experienced it. For, as she put it, "Faith is nothing else but a right understanding and trust of our being, that we are in God and God, whom we do not see, is in us."[24]

Though she underwent significant personal suffering (a major illness that almost killed her before those first revelations), she was the great purveyor of hope. From the confines of her sepulchre-like anchorhold, she urged those who were struggling with life to "notice [Christ] did not say you will not be tempted. He did not say you will not be travailed. He did not say you will not be disquieted. But he did say, 'You will not be overcome.'"[25]

Thus it is no surprise that Julian of Norwich's most lasting legacy has been the saying "All shall be well, all shall be well, and all manner of thing shall be well."[26] She had an unshakable faith in the love and protection of God, a faith so deep that when she finally passed physically from the world, it was apparently a quiet and peaceful transition. Her grave itself, in the tradition of anchoresses, was left unmarked and today is no longer even identifiable. History provides only the scantest record of her deliberately anonymous life here on earth.

My favorite of her sayings seems especially apt for those of us who are aging, who are struggling with the most difficult challenges of all: grief, loss, and the realization of impending death. To one of her visitors, a spiritual seeker plagued by dramatic emotionality, Julian says, "The Holy Ghost makes a soul to be stable and steadfast. You see how we can be shaken, moved about like a cloth in the wind. And doubting moves us like a flood moves to the sea. But God comes with compassion, and his love for us is unending. We discover a rest in the soul."[27]

Or, as Jesus put it thirteen hundred years before Julian, "Do not be afraid, little flock, for it is your Father's good pleasure to give you the kingdom" (Luke 12:32).

❧

The first indicator that my stalwart Uncle Lowell was beginning to fail came in the form of a heart attack he managed to ignore for more than three weeks. He was in his early eighties by then, no longer farming. (The land was being cultivated by a neighbor.) By the time he got around to seeing a doctor, he'd come through the trickiest phase of recovery, but tests showed he was still in grave peril. So, after extracting a promise that he could return to the farm to recuperate, he underwent the same surgery my dad had gone through more than twenty years earlier: a quintuple bypass. The operation had not been enough to save my father, who died in his late sixties. Lowell, however, not only came through it, but also determinedly brought himself back up to speed by doing laps through the old farmhouse.

A few winters later, however, he went outside to feed his cat and fell sideways off the icy backdoor steps. He knew that if he lay outside for more than a few minutes, he'd freeze to death. So he army-crawled his way up the steps, through the door, and up another flight of stairs to the kitchen. He told me later that once he got out of the cold, he might have rested a little, except that he knew he'd done some major damage and would soon be in shock if he wasn't already. Lying there on the bare kitchen floor, pouring icy sweat, he studied the phone on the wall, wondering how in the world he was going to get it down and make that call.

But he did, though nobody, including him, knows quite how, and soon he was undergoing an hours-long surgery for fractures of the hip and pelvis, followed by a six-month stay in a local rest home. Nobody wanted to break the bad news that even if he were eventually allowed to go back to the farm, he'd no longer be driving. That he'd have to hire someone to do what he'd always done on his own: cleaning, cooking, shopping, and mowing. That even though up till now he managed to maintain a semblance of the life lived by his parents and grandparents and great-grandparents before him, he was no longer going to be able to do all that. It would, in fact, be a miracle if he could simply keep himself from falling again.

Secretly, his relatives hoped he would not be allowed to return. No matter that Uncle Lowell was making a marvelous, even miraculous, recovery. No matter that he showed every sign of once again thwarting death. He was eighty-seven. He lived alone in the country. Winters were hard out there. It wasn't safe, and everyone agreed that even if he got to go back, it was only a matter of time until something worse happened. But Lowell wanted to go home, and finally the doctor decided that he could.

One of my Minnesota nieces got married in December of the following year. At the reception dinner afterwards, I was seated next to my intrepid Uncle Lowell, now eighty-eight. His massive, work-swollen hands were so crippled with arthritis that he struggled to cut his meat. The rest of him was shrunken down to nothing. Yet we chatted companionably as we ate, and it hit me once again that here was my last precious living link to my father.

Then I noticed that Uncle Lowell's head was down, his shoulders heaving. Was he choking? I patted him on the back, and he turned his face, peering up at me. "I can't speak," he mouthed. And I realized that his lips were already turning blue. I stood up, grabbed Mike by the shoulder, and said, "Can you do the Heimlich?" Then I rushed through the crowded room, calling out, "Doctor! Is anyone here a doctor!" and three guys in their wedding best made a beeline for our table.

Miraculously, my uncle once again managed to cheat death, but during those frighteningly long moments, it had finally hit me that no one, even the redoubtable Lowell, is invincible. He'd tried his best to hang on to his earthly paradise, to be a good steward of the hard-won land, to carry on the family quest for the sake of the living and the honor of the dead. He'd given the farm his all, singlehandedly holding back the march of time with his commitment to doing things in the old, physically exhausting but tenderly mindful way, the beautiful way I'd so fallen in love with as a child. But this was all coming to an end now, and as much as it grieved me, I knew what I needed to do as soon as I could bring myself to do it.

The morning after the wedding, I found him pawing through my suitcase, looking for his clothes. I could tell he was baffled—wasn't this bedroom at my cousin's house the one he usually stayed in when he visited? I gently steered him back to his own luggage down the hall, dug around until I found his trousers, and held them out to him. Mutely, he stared back at me, and I realized that, between the heart attack, the fractured hip, being eighty-eight, and the near-death experience at the banquet table the night before, he simply couldn't get those pants on by himself.

So I knelt down while he steadied himself against my shoulder, and together we got those skinny legs inside that warm wool. Then we pulled everything up and I stepped back so he could zip the fly on his own. But that wasn't happening either, and I could see by the helplessness on his face that he was already heading away from us, on his way to a new world entirely, whether or not any of us, especially me, was ready for the end of this very long and admirable run.

"Say," he said in his quaint Norwegian bachelor farmer way. "You don't suppose you could help me zip these things up, could you?" Which I did, blinking back surreptitious tears and praying for the ability to accept what couldn't be changed. Counting on Julian in her anchorhold, with her years-long practice of *memento mori*, to know what she was talking about: that "all shall be well, and all shall be well, and all manner of thing shall be well."

7
Appreciating

*You need not cry out very loud. He is nearer to us than we are
aware. And we do not always have to be in church to be with
God. We may make an oratory of our heart so we can, from
time to time, retire to converse with Him in meekness,
humility, and love. Everyone is capable of such familiar
conversation with God, some more, some less. He knows what
we can do.*[28]
—*Brother Lawrence (c. 1614–1691)*

Though nowadays I mostly wake up in a state of peaceful anticipation, it was not always this way. As my first spiritual mentor once told me, "You were one of the angriest young women I'd ever met." And though I was shocked when he said it, I had to admit he was right. For a number of years during my late twenties and thirties, I simmered most of the time.

What was I so angry about? Lots of things. A long list of bad decisions I was sure had held me back. Grudging guilt over the destruction I'd wreaked in other people's lives. Disillusionment. Dreams deferred. Secret despair. God's failure to banish all sin and suffering from the world. And (conversely, if completely illogically) God's failure to exist at all. If someone had asked me then what my view of life had come to be, I would have said something like this: "The ocean is big and we are small, and we're on our own in a leaky boat with broken oars." For a time, I really believed this.

The anger did not dissipate once Mike and I married; if anything, it grew worse. We were still living through the guilty aftermath of our divorces. We were drowning in legal fees. And no matter how hard we worked to make our kids happy, they were not—not with their new step-siblings, not with Mike and me, and not with their TV-less life in the country. Neither were we particularly happy with each other—my new spouse and I. Though we had been to hell and back to be together, now that we were here on this land covered in tumbleweeds and shaggy eucalyptus, we could both see what lay ahead for us: decades of unceasing labor.

Meanwhile, I was already thirty-five and didn't yet have a college degree. I hadn't yet published a novel, something I'd dreamed of doing since I was seven years old. And we were in a lot of debt, which meant I needed to keep working in the kind of going-no-place job I'd held for years. I felt both stifled and frantic, and this seemed particularly crass on my part, considering how much Mike and I had sacrificed to be together. So I kept it to myself, though according to my perceptive mentor, the suppressed anger was lighting me up like a radiation leak.

However, one day while walking the fenceline, I met our neighbor Pat. I liked her immediately, which was an unusual response from me during that secretly disgruntled time. I liked Pat's muddy leather work boots and her long hair twisted into a loose knot the bleached wheat color of fieldstone or dry pasture grass. I liked the way she squinted against the sunlight and the blue flash of her eyes when she laughed. She was in her mid-sixties, thirty years older than I was, and had lived on the eight acres next door for nearly two decades. Her husband was an inventor, and now that their two sons were grown and gone, she spent her time raising horses and pygmy angora goats, plus a motley assortment of dogs and cats. In fact, if I was interested, she could line me up with a good kitten.

I passed on the kitten—thanks to our quest to win over the kids, we'd already taken on way too many of these—but when Pat asked if I'd like to ride with her sometime, I said that yes, I'd love to. For in spite of my distressingly long and ever-growing to-do list, I wanted to be spending more time with this woman. There was something about her I found healing. And during the next five years and despite all the obstacles, we did indeed develop a friendship. She never failed to call when I was most snowed under, and even though it always felt like the worst possible moment to go riding in the hills, it was of course the thing I most needed to do.

She always rode her pretty brown Arab mare, Mujani, and I rode Mujani's elegant but frisky daughter, Sam. We'd wind our way through fields of poppies and blue lupine, or along banks of coastal scrub and oaks. Or we'd head west, toward the sea. During those years we could go for a long time without having to cross through one of the new housing developments that were starting to proliferate on the ocean-facing hillsides. When we did have to cut through one of these construction zones, Sam, always the drama queen, would invariably begin to snort and dance as soon as her hooves hit the slippery asphalt, and Pat worried that the horse would throw me.

We would ride for hours, sometimes talking but often in a friendly silence that did me immeasurable good. By then I knew that Pat's brilliant husband had entered into a long decline. I knew that her equally brilliant sons both lived far away and that she missed them. I knew she had grandchildren she adored and that she longed to see them more often. Like anyone her age, she'd already lost dear friends and had to be thinking about the future. When her husband died, would she be able to stay on the land? Would she have to

give up her horses and the clouds of wild birds who found sanctuary at her feeders? Yet she never alluded to any of this and, given my
propensity toward fretful stewing, I wondered how she'd acquired
this curiously untroubled air. However that had happened, I found
it rejuvenating to be in her presence.

Meanwhile, Mike recognized that at least part of my frustration
had to do with unrealized aspirations. Despite our debt and the
responsibilities that came with this large stepfamily, he urged me to
register for classes at the university where I worked. Thus, in my
late thirties, I finally returned to school. During a general education
course on ethics, I began to catch glimpses of myself—guilty, resentful, and self-pitying—and I was appalled. My ethics professor, who
was to become my spiritual mentor during those early years of finding my way back to faith, introduced me to Janet, his Catholic wife,
and she in turn introduced me to the Hermitage. In the presence
of the monks, I began to experience the same aura of peacefulness I
always felt when I was with Pat. Not that I yet had an ounce of it
myself—that would not come until I got on top of my anger.

Brother Lawrence, a simple seventeenth-century Carmelite monk
who was born into one of the bloodiest eras in European history,
puts his finger on the specific spiritual obstacle that was getting in
my way. Anger is a passion, and all passions, if we let them reign
unchecked, have the power to derail us. Even at a low boil, anger
tends to become all-absorbing, which means we cannot see much
beyond it. Caught up in our own drama, he says, we become blind,

and "Blind as we are, we hinder God and stop the flow of his graces."[29]

Not that we don't need anger; it is our God-given response to the threat of evil. In its purest and most noble state, it rouses us and fills us with courage we normally don't have. It enables us to defend the weak and innocent, stand up for justice, and resist the subtle *logismoi* that lead to nihilistic despair. Anger is like Pat's Great Pyrenees dog, who will fight coyotes to the death to protect her goats. But if this formidable white dog were not so well-trained, it could easily turn on the herd and wreak destruction. The dog of anger, warn the desert fathers, must be disciplined or it will quickly become lethal.

The anger that so often accompanies aging tends to be different, more like the peevish irascibility of cranky old men than the righteous fury of the battlefield hero. But it's not just men who get cranky. Any one of us can recall a grandmother or great-aunt whose diatribes caused us younger folks to roll our eyes and quietly leave the room. According to these angry elders, the world was going to hell in a handbasket. And it didn't help to argue with them. They were neither interested in being convinced otherwise nor in becoming happier. They were tired, and getting riled up made them feel more alive, so their chronic dissatisfaction became the driving force behind almost all they said and did.

What is it about getting old that makes some of us so grumpy? Probably many of the same disappointments that fueled my secret frustration during those early years of my marriage to Mike. But with old age, there is far less chance of changing our circumstances. If we've never gotten to go to college by the time we are eighty, we are probably not going. If we've never experienced the satisfaction of creative work, we are not going to enjoy it at this point. Now that we are old, it feels as though we are trapped in place, reluctant witnesses to a life already lived, with no power to stave off the consequences of our unfortunate choices.

What are some practical steps we can take to resist getting caught by simmering frustration during the aging process? First, we can spend some time honestly searching our souls for "hot spots"—thoughts that cause an emotional rush that seems excessive. Bud, my father-in-law, for example, has a hot spot named Nick, a dishonest man he worked with nearly fifty years ago who deliberately undermined Bud's own standing in the company. As long as Nick remains unforgiven, Bud is susceptible to irritable outbursts whenever that hot spot gets touched—often by something that seems completely unrelated. It's not only buried relationship problems that cause uncontrollable emotional rushes, however; it can also be unrealized dreams, a conviction that life has treated us unfairly, or a physical disability with which we've never come to terms.

Second, we can take this bundle of hot spots to a priest or pastor or even a trusted friend and lay them out on the table, discussing them as openly and thoroughly as possible, then asking for prayer. Once we've shared these secret sensitive areas with somebody else, we've broken the old thought pattern; we've made ourselves accountable. That can help break their hold over us.

Finally, we can begin to practice gratitude. It's almost impossible to be grumpy about life if we are constantly saying "thank you" inside. But we don't confine ourselves to being grateful only for the things that please us or make us feel better; we learn to say thank you for what seems difficult, unfair, or painful, too. How? We begin the practice of gratitude with the assumption that God is with us, no matter what, and through learning to appreciate life, however it comes to us, we are slowly opening ourselves to a greater and greater awareness of his presence.

Once Janet introduced me to the Hermitage, I began going on my own. It was peaceful there, and I felt like I could finally think through some of the issues that were fueling my stubborn anger. I found Brother Lawrence's *The Practice of the Presence of God* in the bookstore, and it became one of the most helpful books I read during this time, perhaps because he knew firsthand about the devastation that occurs when rage goes unchecked. As a young poverty-stricken French peasant, he joined the army out of desperation and wound up serving as a soldier in the brutal Thirty Years War, fought mostly on what is now German soil. Armies in those days were left to their own devices, which meant they were often reduced to decimating the surrounding countryside in order to eat.

Trapped in a violent situation not of his own making, Lawrence began to sink into despair. But then his attention became fixed on a bare-branched tree, and the thought came to him that despite its current bleak aspect, it would soon begin to bud, then leaf out, then produce fruit—all by the providential grace of God. Decades later, he told the man who would become his spiritual biographer that "this view had perfectly set him loose from the world, and kindled in him such a love for God, that he could not tell whether it had increased in above forty years that he had lived since."[30]

When he sustained a grievous spinal injury, he was released from service and worked as a laborer before entering a Discalced Carmelite monastery in Paris, where he lived for the rest of his long life. Despite his lameness, his chronic pain, and his low station within the monastic community (most of his life he was relegated to the kitchen, then became the official repairer of old sandals), Brother Lawrence resolved never to forget the revelation granted him. Though he dutifully strove to follow the Carmelite schedule of prayer, including the hours set aside for private devotion, he soon found that too much thinking about method was confusing him. Instead, he began to use these hours simply to dwell on God and how thankful he was for God's mercy and grace. Though at first this was difficult (like all of us who've ever tried to focus, his mind was prone to wander), Brother Lawrence soon realized that he could ask God to help him in this endeavor. If he himself failed, as in his weakness he inevitably would, it was a waste of time to wallow in guilt. It was much more important simply to ask for forgiveness and get back to the task at hand.

The trick was to pay attention to his thinking. Just as the desert dwellers learned to "watch the thoughts" and "guard the heart," Brother Lawrence taught himself to notice what his mind was doing in order to keep it focused on God. But he found that this worked only if he kept to the vow he made when he first joined the monastery: to voluntarily renounce all thoughts and actions, even harmless and seemingly innocuous little desires and pleasures, that did not help maintain this state of concentrated focus. He understood from the beginning that in this effort we need to be gentle with ourselves. We should never put any "violent constraint upon ourselves" but instead "do our business faithfully, without trouble or disquiet, recalling our mind to God mildly and with tranquility, as often as we find it wandering from him."[31]

Thus, he developed the habit of thinking of God every few moments, all day long, whether he was procuring supplies or cooking or repairing other people's sandals. Brother Lawrence was convinced that if he lived in a state of constant surrender to the will of his Father, especially during times of trouble and pain (or in my case, anger), God would never abandon him and thus he had nothing to fear. Difficulties did not matter, and in fact, they could actually increase the flow of grace. As he writes to a suffering fellow religious, "Adore him in your infirmities," for "love sweetens pain."[32]

Also, such willing surrender will bring with it a "holy freedom" and unutterable joy. Like the great desert elders before him, the more Brother Lawrence practiced the presence of God, the more he experienced the fullness of grace. He discovered that the habit of continually referring everything back to the Creator opens our eyes to the beauty and goodness of his creation. We reorient ourselves around a new center, and in this shimmering light, old complaints, disappointments, and grudges are revealed for what they are—mistaken notions about what is and is not vital to our well-being.

～～～

At some point during those years of visiting the Hermitage, reading the words of great contemplatives such as Brother Lawrence, and learning to pray again, my anger began to subside. Though there were many reasons for its demise (the prodding of my spiritual mentor, the happy influence of Fr. Bernard and my other monk friends, the ameliorating effect of time), being friends with Pat, a woman who radiated gratitude, was equally important. Since our last ride together long ago, when frisky Sam tossed her aristocratic head with such a magnificent flourish that she caught me in the chin with the buckle of her halter and nearly broke my jaw, we continue to enjoy each other's company. I give Pat jars of homemade olallieberry jam; she gives me good lines on kittens. I sit in her dining room with one of her Chihuahuas in my lap; she sits with my little granddaughter in hers.

Through these nearly thirty years of friendship, I've watched Pat weather the loss of her husband, long months of recuperation from a fall that broke both arms, and the tragic death of a beloved grandson. I've wondered where she gets her strength and steady good humor. Though she knows all about my faith—has even read my books—she's never spoken of her own, and, respecting her privacy, I've never questioned her about that. As Brother Lawrence says, we do not need to be in a church to talk with God. What I do know is this. In nearly three decades of friendship, I've rarely heard Pat utter a negative word. I've even wondered if, long ago, she made a private vow to never speak ill of the world. However it came about, I'm convinced that Pat's deep appreciation for life did not happen accidentally but has been the result of a disciplined practice of "watching the thoughts" and refusing to allow anger through the door.

If so, the practice has made her brave. A couple of years ago, after undergoing months of severe pain, she made the decision to have a hip replacement. When she told me, I had to hide my shock. She was eighty-eight, and I was afraid that the anesthesia would cause problems for her later, or that she might not be able to walk again, or that she'd go into a post-surgical downward spiral. But she was firm. The pain was so bad that she couldn't walk anyway, and she missed being able to visit her goats or sit outside among the whirling flocks of birds at the feeders.

Five days after the surgery, I went to see her at the rehabilitation center. She was sleeping when I arrived, so I sat quietly in a chair. When she woke, she looked over at me and smiled.

"How are you?" I asked.

"Pretty good," she said.

"Are they giving you something for the pain?"

"Oh, they tried, but after one pill I said forget it, I don't want to lie here all drugged up. I'd rather have a clear mind."

I was flabbergasted. "Pat," I said. "You are something else."

She laughed her merry laugh. "Remember when that naughty horse of mine cut open your chin?"

I fingered the scar, then tipped my head back so she could see.

"When I looked back and saw that blood all over the front of you, I thought I was going to fall off Mujani."

"*You?*" I said. "What about *me?*"

"The sad part was that I couldn't invite you riding again. I really missed that."

"You couldn't? Why not?"

She smiled again and shook her head, and I realized that her failing husband, by then in a state of nervous fragility, must have put his foot down. No more trail rides. Somebody's going to get more than a banged-up chin out there. Somebody's going to *really get hurt*.

"But we sure had fun while it lasted."

"We did," I said. And we exchanged a look of deep and grateful satisfaction.

8
Befriending

Well, my treasure, have you come? The Lord bless you! Be our guest for a time.[33]
—*Seraphim of Sarov (1759–1833)*

Along with the other reasons Mike and I had for buying four acres when we got married nearly thirty years ago was one I didn't like to acknowledge: country living provided us with a hideout. The semi-isolation gave us a way to start over without being haunted by the ghosts of broken relationships. True, Mike had been teaching in our new area for many years already, but he'd never actually lived there before. As for me, I knew almost nobody and intended to keep it that way for a while. Better to concentrate on our fledgling marriage and stepfamily, I told myself, than to race right out and try to make new friends. And aside from next-door-neighbor Pat, I managed to stay incommunicado for a good long time.

Almost fifteen years, in fact. I knew other people up and down the street enough to wave hi when they passed me on the road. But though I'd been to a block party or two and had attended the annual white-elephant Christmas gift exchange, a decade and a half after we moved there, I was still "in" the neighborhood though not "of" it. Where was I instead? Driving back and forth to the university campus where I got my bachelor's and then master's degrees. Teaching. Shepherding the kids to and from their school near the college. And, whenever I could pull it off, holed up in my office at home, writing like a fiend.

Mike's situation was quite different. After so many years on the job, he knew every kid in town, along with most of their parents. A number of these folks lived along our country road, and he considered them not only friends but also members of his community. Long before he finally retired, he'd acquired a large group of buddies I affectionately referred to as the "chainsaw gang." These were big men who had lived on land like ours for years and knew how to do just about everything that needed to be done. They cut down trees, split firewood, and built fences together. They repaired roofs, painted barns, and poured concrete. They even picked grapes and made serious amounts of wine.

Naturally, whenever this helpful crew happened to be working at our place, I cooked for them. I felt comfortable with this bunch; they were so different from the voluble male professors I was used to. But they were Mike's friends, not mine. Never did I think of myself as part of the larger community, which included these men, their wives, and their kids who, unlike ours, had grown up together in the village.

But then things changed. As the unbridgeable gap between life as it was lived at the Hermitage and life on my big secular campus grew steadily more obvious, I began to think about leaving the university. I'd be fifty soon, and I could take an early retirement. What would I do? I decided I'd live in the spirit of St. Benedict. I would spend a lot more time in the orchard and garden. I'd pray while I was working. And I would write.

Mike was one hundred percent behind this plan and offered to build me a writing studio if only I would quit teaching. I could not think of anything I'd love more, yet the break with my current life would still be wrenching. That teaching job had been hard-won. And I would miss some special people, friends I would see far less often if I no longer worked on campus. But finally I decided to do it.

What I had never thought about, however, was that my "special status" when it came to the social life of the neighborhood would no longer hold once I was home full-time. Instead of being Mike's busy wife, too engrossed in her work to show up at barbeques and birthday parties, I was now presumably "free." Like Mike's longtime buddy group, there was a tight network of community wives out there, women who raised their babies together and who were now swapping grandchild photos. A few of them had already called to invite me to functions I couldn't yet fathom attending. But they'd all known one another for so long; how could I ever fit in? More to the point, hadn't I resigned my teaching job in search of greater solitude?

Though nobody, including Mike, put an ounce of actual pressure on me, I let myself become nervous and self-defensive. What good would it do to divest myself of one set of social obligations only to dive headfirst into another? And let's face it, if my campus colleagues had thought me odd (all those strange monastic proclivities), what would these "normal" people think? I felt exposed and in need of some defense. I tried to make Mike understand. I love your chainsaw guys, I said, but I hardly know their wives. We couldn't possibly have anything in common.

How do you know? he asked—you've never spent enough time with them to find out. But stubbornly I told myself that I had quit teaching to think and pray, not to do whatever it was these women did together.

∽∼∽

We are moving my mom into her new apartment. After forty years in the old house in a city two hundred miles away, she is justifiably apprehensive. Like a freshman in college just moving into the dorms, she knows absolutely no one; yet, from now on, these will be the people with whom she shares her life. Will she have anything in common with her neighbors? Is it possible to make good friends when you are already in your eighties? Though she doesn't say much about it, I can tell she is nervous.

One hint is that she, an inveterate nonshopper, asks one of my sisters to help her pick out a couple of new sweaters before she makes her debut in the dining hall. The weather is cooler in our area, and on our exploratory trips to the apartment complex, she has noticed that most of the women wear stylish cardigans rather than the windbreakers she prefers. It's clear that her newcomer status has made her touchingly vulnerable, and we siblings agree that it's important for us to help her get past the hump; then we'll quietly disappear so that she can make her adjustment in private.

The day of the move we surround her with family, including the little great-grandchildren she so rarely sees but who will now be living much closer to her. Big grandsons help muscle her furniture up three flights. Granddaughters bring potted plants and welcome cards. Sons-in-law hang pictures and extra shelves. And after we're done, all of us lounge around until it feels almost like the old family house again. The expression on her face is a complicated mixture of gratitude, exhaustion, relief, and doom. Dinnertime is nigh, and the moment of truth is upon her.

But then there is a knock at the door, the tentative tap-tap of a stranger. We open it up, and there stands Betty, a neighbor just down the way, and she's here, she explains, to welcome Mom to the community and to invite her to join the "six-o'clocks" in the dining hall that night. "The six-o'clocks," she tells us, "like to eat a little later than the five-thirties, but you should feel free to do whatever you want. Some people just get hungry earlier!" Betty, who has a sweet face and red hair and is quite a bit taller than my short mother but obviously of the same generation, beams at us. "What a nice big family!" she adds.

Mom, who is staring up at her like a shy little girl, has not yet said a word. I gesture at the sofa. "Betty," I urge, "please sit down."

"Oh, no, no, no." She flaps her hands as if to make herself go poof and says, "I know what it's like, just moving in. We've all been through it here. You must be exhausted. I'll leave you to your unpacking. But I just wanted to let you know you're invited to join us any time you'd like."

All eyes swing back to Mom, who is still standing mutely in the doorway, now looking a mite desperate. I suddenly realize she was probably hoping to put off this moment for another week or so, to perhaps eat on alternate nights with Mike and me and then with my sister Gail and her husband until she feels really, truly ready to meet her new community face-to-face. Kind-hearted Betty has, without intending to, just invalidated this option, and I wonder what Mom, wiped out as she is, will do or say next. But right when we think that Betty will have to depart without an answer, Mom blurts out, "I'm going to have dinner with my grandchildren tonight, but how about if I join you tomorrow?"

"It's a date!" says Betty gaily. "I'll come pick you up!" And off she goes, a woman we later find out is legally blind, though apparently still able to read faces. Indeed, to read them well enough to break through the universal dread suffered by any stranger who can only hope for a welcome but who can't make it happen on her own.

The Benedictine rule of hospitality is rooted in this deep human need to be included, to find a home among caring neighbors, and to know that we can turn to others for help. For centuries, the Benedictines have offered physical and spiritual shelter to the pilgrim and the stranger. Their practice of hospitality has its foundation in Jesus' startling declaration that what we do for others, we do for him: "For I was hungry and you gave me food, I was thirsty and you gave me something to drink, I was a stranger and you welcomed me, I was naked and you gave me clothing, I was sick and you took care of me, I was in prison and you visited me" (Matthew 25:35–36). Such hospitality opens more than the door of the monastery; it has the power to break through the hardpan of a heart in long drought. Desert father literature is rife with spectacular hospitality stories, including elders embracing would-be robbers or murderers—generous welcomes that were sometimes followed by the transformation of former evil-doers into new brothers in Christ.

Yet hospitality is only part of the picture. Jesus calls us to make an even greater investment than this in our fellow human beings. We are to love them as we love ourselves. We are to offer ourselves in friendship, to invite them into our lives. We are to give up some of our own freedom—the freedom to get bored and abandon the relationship or to get frustrated with their complexities—so that we can become a kind of champion, in the old sense of "loyal defender," of their souls. When we befriend people, we affirm their value as persons. The Catholic philosopher Josef Pieper defines this kind of love as a message conveyed: "It's good that you exist!"[34]

However, this is easier said than done. Let's face it; many (if not most) people are not inherently lovable. What are some ways that we can begin to practice the discipline of befriending while still being practical about our own limitations and the limitations of other people? We can spend a little time each day meditating on all the ways we've been loved in spite of our nasty habits, negative attitudes, or unrelenting bossiness. In my case, the list of those who have bestowed undeserved love on me is wonderfully, if depressingly, long. Mike, who has stood loyally beside me through thick and thin, heads the lineup. When I find myself coming up with excuses for why I can't befriend this person or that, all I have to do is think about Mike and what he has deliberately "looked past" in me to be able to love me the way he does.

We can go back through our memories, looking for times when we've been in the lonely stranger position ourselves. How did it feel to be overlooked and ignored? Who, if anyone, came to our rescue? And if somebody did, then how did it feel to be made welcome when we were at our low point? In what ways can we pay back the debt we accrued when somebody extended the hand of friendship at a time we really needed it? A meditation along these lines can quickly put things into proper perspective.

And we can pray for the ability to love better. Love is called a theological virtue because in an important sense it is beyond our power to develop on our own; it must be infused through grace. What we can do is ask, and ask again, for this great gift of a loving spirit.

The eighteenth-century Orthodox saint Seraphim of Sarov spent decades as a hermit in near-total solitude before finally emerging to become one of the great befrienders in Christian history. He had a special feeling for laypeople, often addressing them as "my joy," "my treasure," "mother," "father," and "your Godliness."[35] Sometimes he actually bowed down to the ground before them and kissed their hands, peasants included. He assured them that he did not consider his monastic life in any way superior to theirs. In fact, they had their own spiritual path to forge through the thorny thickets of marriage and family.

One of the most important manuscripts concerning St. Seraphim's teachings is the journal of disciple N. A. Motovilov the Elder. It sheds some light on Seraphim's strikingly loving relationships with so many total strangers whose lives were entirely different from his own:

> Thus, my son, whatever you ask of the Lord God you will receive, if only it is for the glory of God for the good of your neighbour, because what we do for the good of our neighbour He refers to His own glory. And therefore He says: "All that you have done unto one of the least of these, you have done unto Me" (Matthew 25:40). And so, have no doubt that the Lord God will fulfill your petitions, if only they concern the glory of God or the benefit and edification of your fellow men.[36]

Everything he did was fueled by the burning desire to spread Christ's love to the world. He once urged a priest, "Sow, Fr. Timon, sow! Sow everywhere the wheat which has been given to you. Sow on the good ground, sow on the sand, sow even on the rock, sow by the wayside, sow among the thorns. Somewhere or other it will sprout, and grow, and produce fruit, even though not soon."[37] When the superior of a monastery complained that he was concerned about preserving the morals of his monks and asked what method he should use, St. Seraphim said, "By charity, making their work easier, and not by wounds. . . . Give them food and drink, be just! The Lord is tolerant (with you). You, too, forgive."[38]

The effect of this great befriender on the people who sought him out was profound. Many went away sobbing, though no longer in despair but in relief and even joy. Others felt as though they'd received an infusion of grace and found a new delight in living. All of them—even those whose sinful hearts he'd read—left comforted, understanding that they were no longer alone. As with the crowds around Jesus, those pressing in to see St. Seraphim and receive a word from him were sometimes vast. He often spent sixteen or eighteen hours a day listening to people and giving counsel and blessing. Yet despite this grueling schedule, many spoke of the unearthly radiance of his joyful face.

My own befriending took place in a way St. Seraphim, with his love and respect for laypeople, would have approved of—it came in the form of a handcrafted gift. What I did not realize during those first disoriented months after early retirement was the extent of my loneliness. Once I quit teaching, I could no longer define myself by what I did. I felt like a stranger to myself and everyone around me. Though this was a necessary stage on the spiritual journey, it was far more painful than I could admit, even to myself. I felt isolated at times, even friendless. And aside from Mike and our far-flung kids—apart from the monks when I could get to them—there was nobody on whom it felt safe to lean.

Then our oldest daughter, Andrea, got engaged, and she and her fiancé asked if they could have the wedding on our property. It wouldn't be large—only two hundred twenty-five people or so. And it would be so great if their friends from all over the country could camp out in the barn for a few days afterward. What did we think? Because of course they knew it would take a LOT of work, but everyone would help, wouldn't they?

Of course they would, we told them. Let's do it! And grasping at this unexpected chance to become part of a team once again, I threw myself into the project. Mike's buddies built an outdoor shower for the barn guests and designed and constructed a dance floor in the pasture. But as the months went on and the day approached, I realized that we were going to need more than the chainsaw gang to pull off this event. We were going to need the women, too—those kind-hearted neighborhood wives I was still, in my outsider's mode, holding at bay.

Before I could work up the courage to ask, one of the guys mentioned that his wife was making our daughter a quilt. She was? "Oh, yeah," Joe said. "She does that for all our kids' weddings. You know. It's kind of her thing."

I knew Jeanne was a quilter, but the part that had never crossed my mind was that *our* kids, kids who had not grown up in the neighborhood, would be considered a subset of "all our kids," as in "all our kids' weddings." In essence, Joe was telling me that we—*I*—belonged here after all, that we were part of the community without even knowing it. And our daughter Andrea, no matter how far away she lived, was thereby part of the community, too—and thus deserved one of Jeanne's special wedding quilts.

I had just had the hand of friendship extended to me, the odd, reclusive monk-meister divorcée, wife of the otherwise-normal Mike. And it had been extended in the most exquisite way possible, through the making of a symbolic gift. Jeanne's beautiful quilt could be passed down for generations to come. Thanks in part to her generosity and that of so many other local residents, the young couple themselves would several years later migrate from a distant state to take up new lives in this community.

Meanwhile, warmed and emboldened by the gesture, I called Jeanne to thank her. She asked if we needed some help on the big day, and I admitted that we surely did, and she told me she'd be there and that I should give Mary and the two Carolyns and Kathy and Loxie a call right away. Filled with happy relief, I did call them. And they all said what I might have expected them to say if only I'd gotten to know them years before: We'd love to!

Within the space of a week, thanks to the many befrienders who live in her apartment complex, Mom is already part of her new community. Soon she is having breakfast with Eric and Katie in the morning, going to a morning exercise class, eating dinner with the six-o'clocks (except when she craves a conversation with one of the five-thirties), then playing cards with Aggie in the evening. In no time at all, we—her many children—are reduced to making dates in advance if we want to drop by. Mom is so involved in her new world that it's hard to fit us into her schedule.

One day I go by to have lunch with her, then walk her to the bus stop where she is meeting up with a group from the complex to go on an adventure. As we approach, she puts her hand on my arm to break off our conversation, then heads over to speak with a woman standing off to one side. When she finally comes back, I ask, "One of your buddies?"

"No, she's new. Just moved in from Missouri. She's probably still feeling pretty overwhelmed. So I asked to sit next to her—her name's Vivian—on the bus." Mom looks, if not smug, then downright pleased with herself. She's been in town for less than four months, and here she is, already extending the hand of friendship to a nervous stranger. I'm just as proud of her as she is of herself, and I start to tell her so. But then the bus pulls up, and Mom gives me a wave—toodledoo!—and climbs on board, a grateful-looking Vivian in her wake, looking as though she's just heard those magic words: It's good that you exist!

9
Generating

I began to think I had a mission. . . . Before starting from my
inn in the morning of 26 or 27 May, I sat down on my bed,
and began to sob bitterly. My servant, who had acted as my
nurse, asked what ailed me. I could only answer him, "I have
a work to do in England." [39]
—*John Henry Newman (1801–1890)*

For several years after leaving my teaching career behind, I grappled
with bouts of something close to, but not exactly, depression and
something near to, but not quite, panic. These strange moods were
made worse by the decision to stop writing literary fiction, which
was so deeply intertwined, at least in my own mind, with the academic identity I'd left behind. For nearly a year, I wrote nothing at
all, devoting myself instead to domestic chores like weeding, pick-
ing berries, making soup, and drying apricots. There I'd be, feeling pleased and grateful for the sun, the birdsong, and the cessation
of all striving, when suddenly I'd be teetering on the edge of the
Abyss. These attacks by the spirit of futility came without warning
and always knocked the breath clean out of me. And then, slowly,
I'd recover, a little stronger, a little more settled into this new way of
being, but still wary.

What was going on with me? At times it felt as though I'd gone
crazy. Thank heaven for books, which I devoured during this difficult and obscure passageway between one kind of life and another.

Thank heaven for the cloud of witnesses that surrounded me, people from countless generations before who'd taken the trouble to record their own experiences of the dark patches on the spiritual path. Thank heaven, too, for my lifeline, the Hermitage, and for those particular monks, Fr. Bernard and Fr. Isaiah, who acted as my spiritual guides. Without all of them, those living teachers and long-dead saints, I may have given in to fear and rushed back to the only life I knew—the life of academic striving and artistic ambition—if simply to recover the blessed security of feeling purposeful again.

But for whatever reason (an inability to admit how badly I was struggling? stubbornness? pride?), I did not return to the old life. And finally the darkness began to lift and I began to discern the faintest outlines of what might happen next, which was a new kind of writing, aimed at people like me who were going through something they had no way to understand because our culture no longer understood it and had no place for it. I began to hear the faintest whisper of a calling, one I could not possibly have heard when I was so totally immersed in that other world. I began to discern a purpose not my own at work behind the seeming purposelessness of my days.

For the next many months, I buried myself in the little studio on our pine-covered hill that Mike built for me when I quit teaching. I read and wrote and eventually began to publish new sorts of books. And pretty soon, people were writing back to me, telling me about their lives, and then they were inviting me to speak at their churches, and eventually, at big church conferences. Within five years I could hardly remember that strange dead zone between lives, which had actually not been dead at all but pregnant with possibility. My prayers by this time had become fervent and thankful: "Thank you, God, for giving me the guts to leave my old job. Thank you for providing enough income that I didn't have to go back.

Thank you for freeing me from the seductive tentacles of ambition."
For ambitious I had surely been.

Deep down, however, I was still afraid of that the old competitive Paula. I didn't miss her a bit, and it had been a long grind indeed
to disentangle myself from her influence, but I couldn't yet dismiss
her as a threat, should the right set of circumstances arise. Despite
my spiritual director's assurances that by now it was perfectly safe
for me to write whatever I wanted to, I still couldn't let myself take
the chance. Better to repudiate literary fiction forever than to risk a
relapse into ambitious striving. So instead, I confined myself to the
seemingly ambition-free world of parish speaking and Catholic publishing until, out of the blue, I got a phone call that knocked my
hard-won peace right on its head.

The call was from the director of a Master of Fine Arts in
Creative Writing program. Would I be interested in mentoring graduate writing students?

Aside from the unexpectedness of the offer, what surprised me
most was that I didn't even ask for some time to think about it.
"I'll do it," I said, not mentioning that even my own spiritual director had not yet been able to talk me into writing a short story. No
doubt it helped that the sponsoring university was Christian and
that my students, though they would come from many different religious backgrounds, would be Christian as well. In the end, what
convinced me to say yes so quickly was a reoccurrence of that faint,
whispery, electrifying sensation I'd learned to associate with being
called. What was God asking me to do *now*?

Though it took a while to figure out, I finally saw it. I was being
called to lay my private qualms aside, gird up my loins, and step
into a new role in life. For here was a job that needed doing, one
that only persons of my age—fifty-nine and up—were qualified to

handle. It was time for me to start consolidating what I'd learned, lo these many years, and begin passing it on to an upcoming generation. And in this role, there was no room whatsoever for that old demon of personal ambition.

Only love.

I am sitting in the confession chapel at the Hermitage where Fr. Isaiah and I have just wrapped up another lengthy session—lengthy, because I am always so glad to see him, especially with his official confessor's stole over his shoulders, that my loquaciousness knows no bounds. As is usual after these marathons, we are now leaning back in our chairs, beaming exhaustedly at one another. Then a faint and eerie singing wafts our way. My ears prick up, and I raise an eyebrow at my confessor, who smiles. "Br. Gabriel," he says. "He does that sometimes when he thinks he's alone in the chapel." The singing goes on, breathy and unreal, sometimes from one part of the church and sometimes from another. "He's dancing," adds Fr. Isaiah.

Dancing? Br. Gabriel is the sacristan, which means he is charge of setting things up in the sanctuary before services. He's in his eighties, with some serious heart problems. What in the world is he doing *dancing?*

I soon find out. The next morning between services, I'm in the back of the church, returning a borrowed book to Fr. Robert's mailbox, when suddenly Br. Gabriel, who is very short and looks exactly like I imagine a desert father would look, materializes at my elbow. Though he is usually a man of very few words, today he has something to tell me. So we stand there for fifteen minutes while he speaks to me in his low, rapid voice about mystical prayer. He tells me things, clearly drawn from his nearly fifty years as a contemplative hermit/monk, that I have only read about before. And I realize that this is not a conversation but a teaching. Br. Gabriel is imparting, with some urgency, information he believes I need if I am to continue on this spiritual path. I listen, only half-understanding but trying my best to remember. Then, abruptly, he is done.

What has prompted him to share all this with me? I can only think that somehow, though he could neither see nor hear us the day before, he knew that I was listening as he danced and sang his way throughout the darkened chapel. I can only believe that something larger than either of us thrust us together for this intense quarter of an hour; that for this particular interval, I was meant to be his student and he, my mentor. I can only conclude that this unusual overture by an otherwise silent man has been prompted by the same impulse that drives any of us to pass on what we have learned to a younger generation: love.

~~~~~

How sad that one of the most crippling losses we have suffered during modern times is the dwindling respect for our elders. Our heavy investment in individualism and in developing a unique personal identity means that we can't afford to look backward to the traditions of the past. Thus, where we once turned to the aged for wisdom, we now focus on what's current and new and happening—which means that we focus on youth. Never mind that most teens and twenty-somethings are naive, idealistic, inexperienced, and (sadly) too often prematurely jaded. They can't help but entrance

us. They radiate the kind of energy and beauty we will never have
again. They inspire us to hang onto whatever remnants of youthful-
ness we still possess, even if this means spending thousands of dollars
on plastic surgery and personal trainers and staying in fashion (read,
dressing like a teen). The young embody everything we wish we still
had; the old are simply the bereft.

Thus, the elderly are often the last people we think of as our
natural-born teachers. How could they be? They grew up in different
times, we tell ourselves. The world has totally changed, we say. They
may be quaint, even mildly interesting with all those old walking-to-
school-barefoot-in-three-feet-of-snow stories of theirs, but who can
connect to them in this day and age? Their attitudes are based on
values that have become obsolete. They are irrelevant. Sad, maybe,
but these are the facts.

The aged, however benignly they seem to lean upon those walk-
ers, are not unaware of societal attitudes toward their generation.
They feel the sting of being patronized (we often talk to old people
the same way we talk to toddlers) at the same time they are being
ignored. Many of them deeply resent it. And so, hoping for a little
respect, they harp on the younger generation, scornfully contrast-
ing their own tough childhoods with those of the computer kids.
They criticize young parents for their permissiveness. ("In my day,
my daddy would have hauled me to the woodshed if I acted like
that.") Or they become ingrown, bitter, and envious of those still
in the game, those young upstarts now running the show, from the
government on down.

Some of them simply withdraw, preferring to keep their experiences to themselves or to save them for people their own age, the
only ones who can understand. Hence, the bonding that takes place
in apartment complexes like my mom's; everybody there knows what

it's like to have survived the Depression, World War II, and raising 1960s teenagers. Some older people not only retreat from the wider culture but also deliberately hoard their wisdom, refusing to make it easy for the upcoming generation. ("I learned it the hard way and so can they.") The ultimate result is a Grand Canyon-sized gulf between the very people who should be spending the most time together: wise elders and the young.

One subculture that is still dependent on the wisdom of the aged is monasticism. The survival of the monastic tradition throughout centuries of cultural change has always depended on the ability of its elders to generate spiritual growth in youthful seekers. It is understood that the formation process takes many years and that there are particularly difficult stretches along the way that only someone who's safely navigated them himself has the credentials to address. Not only do older monks enjoy a status in the monastery far higher than they would if they were simply laymen in our youth-oriented society, but also monasticism is inherently backward-looking. It consciously relies on the accumulated wisdom of the long-dead, the voices the wider culture now considers irrelevant.

As important as the elder tradition still is in contemporary monasteries, in ancient days it provided the very structure of monastic life. In the time of the desert fathers, novices were taught to reveal their thoughts and lay open their hearts to a holy man, invariably an old hermit or monk who had himself undergone decades of rigorous ascetical training and by now had seen it all. But he could not guide them through the shoals of temptation simply by relying on his own store of personal experience. His wisdom came from God and his spiritual power from the Holy Spirit. The relationship that developed between an elder and a novice at the beginning of his or her spiritual journey was akin to that of parent and child; the elder took on responsibility for the health of the novice's soul, loving and praying for his new offspring in Christ.

How might this relationship look in modern times, and more important, outside the monastery? Is it still possible, even with our cultural resistance to aging, for those of us who are older and wiser to become "generators" of new spiritual life in the young?

I believe that it is, but with some caveats. Most of us, no matter how hard we may have worked or how much suffering we may have borne, have not undergone much conscious spiritual formation ourselves. If we are to generate growth in the young, we must at the very least first be willing to plumb our own spiritual depths. We must get to "know ourselves" in the way that Socrates meant this—know our particular temptations, our strengths, our "weak planks." Even after all that, we must have something of worth to teach, and we must be called to teach it. Our teaching must be free of egoistic concerns, especially the desire to be important in young people's lives. And—most important—it must be fueled by love.

One of my favorite examples of a true "generator" who adhered to these principles is the brilliant Oxford scholar John Henry Newman. Setting out to explain his theological position in the face of severe opposition, he wrote a spiritual autobiography, *Apologia Pro Vita Sua,* that in his time—the mid-nineteenth century—resulted in the revitalization of an almost-dead Roman Catholicism on English shores. The story of his evolving faith became a spiritual template for countless university students, including the brilliant young Jesuit poet Gerard Manley Hopkins, who were seeking a full-scale commitment to a Christianity more ancient and more challenging than the socially approved forms of Protestantism and Anglicanism of their day.

Newman's road to Catholicism was long, painful, and convoluted, and at times, he was understandably filled with self-doubt. England was still recovering from the bloody, religiously fueled conflicts of the past three centuries, including the English Civil War that had pitted the Anglican King Charles I against a pro-Calvinist Parliament in the 1640s. Charles, suspected of trying to remake the Church of England on Catholic lines, actually holed up in Oxford for the winter of 1642, then made it his base for the duration of the war. The university community thus had a personal stake in the long-running religious feuds that had torn English society apart. In Newman's day, anybody who dared to profess sympathy for Roman Catholic doctrine or practices risked major consequences, from having his patriotism questioned to having his Christian identity impugned to even losing his job.

What was perhaps most difficult for Newman was that his spiritual development did not unfold in a straightforward way but went through several different, and seemingly contradictory, stages. Though very early in his life he was convinced of the rightness and vigor of Evangelicalism, by the time he was in his late twenties, he'd become an Anglican priest. During this period, he saw Anglicanism as the perfect vehicle for keeping alive the most important aspects of ancient Christianity, and thus he became involved in the tumultuous Oxford Movement of the 1830s, which attempted to reform an English church grown increasingly liberal. The "Tractarians," as they were called, tried to prove that the Church of England provided a third way to God, neither Roman nor Greek, but united to each through a common root in the original church instituted by Christ.

Though Newman did not set out to write for students, he understood that in them lay the potential for religious growth and change: "Living movements do not come from committees. . . .

Universities are the natural centres of intellectual movements."[40] By the end of the 1830s, Oxford students were flocking to his sermons. Given his obvious influence over the young intellectuals of England, he became an increasingly controversial figure and the particular target of those who saw in the Movement an attempt to convert the English youth to "papistry."

In time, Newman had to admit to himself that his accusers were right about one thing, at least; he had become a Catholic in all but name. He knew that if he were to follow his conscience, he must bid farewell to his beloved Oxford. He knew that he would never again be taken seriously by his peers, and that cut off from the intellectual community in England, he would be relegated to teaching in some comparatively minor Catholic college. Yet he could do nothing else at this point. And so, at age forty-five, he voluntarily said good-bye to the school he thought he'd serve until old age. He never saw it again, "excepting its spires," as he later wrote to a friend, "as they are seen from the railway."[41]

Twenty years later, a longtime priest now considered a wise old elder by a new generation of religious seekers, he wrote *Apologia Pro Vita Sua*. That the motivating force of his life was love is very clear in the concluding passages. He thanks his Catholic brothers in the Birmingham Oratory, where he has lived for many years. "In you," he says, "I gather up and bear in memory those familiar affectionate companions and counsellors, who in Oxford were given to me, one after another, to be my daily solace and relief, . . . and also those many younger men, whether I knew them or not, who have never been disloyal to me by word or deed."[42]

In a few poignant last lines, he reveals his most cherished dream for the church instituted by Jesus, the church of all Christians: "And I earnestly pray for this whole company, with a hope against hope, that all of us, who once were so united, and so happy in our union, may even now be brought at length, by the Power of the Divine Will, into One Fold and under One Shepherd."[43]

～～～

Despite my conviction that God was calling me back into academic life, I couldn't help but feel a little apprehensive the day I met my first cohort of graduate students. It had been ten years, after all, and the break with university life had been so wrenching. I truly believed I'd left it behind forever and that things were better this way, certainly safer. But now, here we were, these students and I, each of us privately excited and dubious at the same time. How would we be together? Could I possibly be the mentor they were seeking? Would our relationship generate new spiritual growth for us all?

Within that first hour, I knew. They were entrancingly, beautifully young, the same age as my adult children, and they were filled with the kind of hope and energy I no longer had. These were people who could, I was sure, stay up all night, every night, listening to one another read poetry or play the guitar. They could, I was positive, read faster than I could, write with more flair than I ever would, and remember facts that I'd forget as soon as I left the residency. I was momentarily nonplussed. How would I ever keep up with them?

I couldn't and I wouldn't, and this was OK. The role of a "generator" is not to keep up with the young, to try to pass as one of them, to be "cool"; the role is to impart the wisdom they do not yet have. It's to hint at mysteries beyond their ken, as Br. Gabriel did with me. It's to fill them with the courage that only an exemplar like John Henry Newman can convey. It's to stand in the road beside them with one hand on their backs, gently urging them forward, and the other pointing toward a future that only they will see.

10
Blessing

I am convinced that we can choose joy. Every moment we can choose to respond to an event or a person with joy instead of sadness. When we truly believe that God is life and only life, then nothing need have the power to draw us into the sad realm of death. To choose joy does not mean to choose happy feelings or an artificial atmosphere of hilarity. But it does mean the determination to let whatever takes place bring us one step closer to the God of life.[44]
—*Henri Nouwen (1932–1996)*

The irrational anger that characterized my young adult years had its roots in a passionately self-defensive childhood. Some of my earliest memories have to do with defiance: sticking out my tongue at age three because Mom asked me to pick up my toys; telling bold-faced lies about eating all my broccoli when actually I'd just buried it in the garden; whacking my irritating little brother across the face with a baseball mitt and then feeling abused when I got sent to my room without supper. The other (exactly opposite) memories: waving my hand from the front row in second grade to make sure the teacher knew I had the answer; staying afterward to clean the chalkboards so that she would like me best; proudly earning straight A's on my report cards and lavish commendations for my exemplary "citizenship" in the classroom.

Though the behavior at home and at school could not have been more different, the motive was the same: I had a crying need for praise. When it was not forthcoming at the levels I demanded—as it rarely was in our crammed household held together by a frazzled mom—then I made her pay, and pay big. School was my salvation because not only could I rack up endless brownie points with my beaver-like diligence, but I could also use my perfect report cards as proof that my mom's judgment was skewed: *See, I'm not the kid you think I am.*

The only time my "school self" made an appearance at home was when we had relatives in town. My California grandparents made a short visit almost every summer. I had cartloads of cousins, so there was little chance of my standing out in the crowd, but still I tried, worming my way into the spotlight in hopes of hearing what a marvelously good and talented girl I must be. However, my grandparents were not suckers. They had raised six kids of their own during the Depression and had nearly twenty-five grandkids by now, so they were not very easily charmed.

One day a special group of relatives arrived, my cousins from Minnesota who were on their way to Japan. My Uncle Ivan, a Lutheran pastor, had long dreamed of serving in the mission field, and now they were going. They would stay with us for five days, then board a freighter that would take them across the Pacific to this exotic land I'd only read about in school. I was enthralled by their courage and dedication, and I really, really wanted to be able to count myself in their class. So I went into overdrive, hoping for a pat on the back from my august uncle.

But he, too, was impervious to my charm. He was incredibly kind, but his kindness was for everybody. He was wonderfully attentive when you spoke with him, but then again he was attentive to everyone. He was warm, funny, and magnetically attractive (even the neighbor's wary dog could not stay away from him), but you did not have to be especially good to bring that out in him; it was there for the taking. Oddly, however, I did not mind in the least. I was only a child, but already I could feel the difference between "getting my due" and being gratuitously blessed. For this is what Uncle Ivan did; through his very presence, he blessed the world, including spiritually impoverished little me.

The impact he made on my soul had little to do with the amount of actual time I spent in his presence. As it turned out, for most of my childhood, Ivan and his family were in Japan. But on that first Christmas after they sailed, my aunt sent us a box full of small kimonos and teetering velvety sandals on wooden blocks and chopsticks and fans, and I began to dream of becoming a missionary myself, possibly in Africa, possibly in the mode of Albert Schweitzer. If I sacrificed myself in the mission field, maybe I could become really good, as opposed to falsely good in the way my school self was falsely good. Maybe I could become like Uncle Ivan.

After some years, my Japanese cousins came home for a few months' furlough, and Ivan was invited to preach at a big Lutheran church in Hollywood. The whole extended family—grandparents, aunts, uncles, and cousins—piled into cars to hear him. In a happy daze of reflected glory—I was his niece! he was my uncle!—I concentrated with my formidable intensity on his every word. Afterward at the family picnic, I asked him a couple of adult-sounding questions concerning the Japanese economy and the future of Christianity in Asia, and he gave a surprised laugh. "Well, I guess *some*body was listening to me." I beamed, but not because he praised me. He did something better; he wished me well—me, a whole person, mixed with all that bad and good—and he infused me with a new hope for myself and other people.

Many years later, now a retired theology professor living with my Aunt Pauline in Minnesota, Uncle Ivan came back into my life when our son Johnny decided to go to the college where Ivan had taught. Ivan and Pauline housed us when we went on the campus tour, and for the next few years, every time I flew back for choir concerts and graduation. During Johnny's freshman year, while he was still struggling with manfully disguised homesickness (he'd been born and raised in our small California town and never before lived away from his network of local buddies), Ivan, these days looking much like Santa Claus, quietly took him on, offering him an island of sanctuary in the midst of the freshman social whirl.

One December, I locked my keys inside a running rental car in Ivan and Pauline's driveway. Deep snow lay on the ground. It was freezing. Ivan, wearing one of his signature Norwegian sweaters, came chuckling out the door to see what kind of mess I'd gotten myself into. He called a locksmith, waited with me until he got there, and then made sure I got safely on my way. Though he'd never met the locksmith before, he fed him lunch and gave him a counseling session after I was gone; the man was in crisis and needed the kind of blessing only my uncle could bestow.

⁓ᴗᴗᴗ⁓

I am sitting in the small, multiwindowed chapel of a Franciscan friary. The twisted bows of the old coastal oaks outside, some of them nearly touching the ground, remind me of Big Sur. It is 8:15 on a weekday morning, the only time I can come to Mass here, thanks to Sunday duties and good friends at my official church, the much larger St. Pat's. This chapel is simple but strikingly beautiful with its gleaming maple floor, black granite altar, and medieval-looking cherubim candleholders. I love the hush of wind through the oaks, the blue sky beyond them, and the cry of the red-tailed hawks that circle like avenging angels in the troposphere above us. During my normal daily schedule, this is the closest I can come to being at the Hermitage.

Aside from a single friar kneeling in prayer, I am the only person in the church. Then the bell rings, and out comes Fr. Chris. Though we are few, he is garbed in full liturgical vestments, and as he processes alone to the altar, the air in the room seems to brighten and clarify. I wonder about that—why he has this effect, for he always does, on a room already so beautiful. He bows low before the altar, then turns to the two of us and smiles with such welcome in his eyes that instantly I feel weepy. Again, this is how it always is when Fr. Chris offers Mass, and the effect is so consistent and so powerful that on Sundays, I've heard, almost half the people who crowd into this tiny church for the Eucharist are not even Catholic but simply come to be blessed.

Today, he begins in Latin, as he often does, singing parts of the Mass in his burnished tenor. He takes his time, embodying reverence in every gesture, and I know once again why every so often I must come here. By now I have met other holy people besides my Uncle Ivan, but here is one who is actually engaged in an inherently holy ritual—holy times holy, so to speak—and the effect on bystanders is multiplied exponentially. This is the kind of priest Paul must have been envisioning in his letter to Timothy, the kind of priest who has become the living embodiment of the Gospel he preaches and the sacrifice over which he presides: "But as for you, man of God, . . .

pursue righteousness, godliness, faith, love, endurance, gentleness" (1 Timothy 6:11).

As always, I am reduced to a state of helpless gratitude by the end of this Mass. As always, thanks to the transparent holiness of Fr. Chris, I've been doubly and triply blessed.

~~~

The fourth-century pilgrims who made the difficult and dangerous journey into the desert were looking for a similar experience. They were hoping to be blessed by someone who reminded them of Christ. And so they sought out the famous holy ones, who were often abiding in caves or wattle huts, were often bearded and unwashed, were (at least if they were women) living in complete disguise. The prospect of being in the presence of holiness was so enthralling that the first of the great Christian hermits, St. Anthony the Great, has continued to show up in Western art and literature for the past sixteen hundred years.

What does it mean to be holy? The word itself comes from an Old English term, *halig*, which means "whole, entire, uninjured, healthy, sound, or complete." For the desert dwellers, it meant that one had become pure of heart, freed from the incessant demands of the desiring, passionate self. One was no longer ruled by anger, envy, lust, gluttony, vainglory, self-pity, or pride. One's vision was clear. And one's heart was capable of real love, the universal love modeled by Jesus, which meant that one's original nature had been restored.

How was this holiness manifested? The same way it is today: through the spiritual fruits of love, joy, peace, patience, kindness, generosity, faithfulness, gentleness, and self-control (Galatians

5:22–23). When we are in the presence of a holy person, we find ourselves in some way "restored to paradise," as St. Basil puts it, or at the very least, given a glimpse of our true homeland.[45] No wonder we are magnetized; here is the living proof we have been seeking, that we, too, can be transformed. We are inspired, our heads turned, however momentarily, in a whole new direction.

Holy people not only offer us a vision of what might be, but they also infuse us with some of their own goodness. Oxford scholar and author C. S. Lewis says that we are not so much argued into faith, but infected by others' faith. This maxim holds doubly true when we are in contact with holy people. Orthodox theologian Olivier Clément speaks of Christianity as the "religion of faces," and the face of a holy person speaks eloquently of forgiveness, mercy, redemption, grace, and love.[46] Holiness is thus healing, which means we are in some measure liberated from bondage to petty egoism, self-pity, brooding anger, bitter envy, and secret lust simply by being in the presence of someone who is holy.

Are the holy then perfect? Uncle Ivan, who would be horrified to hear himself described as holy, would even more adamantly declare that he is a very imperfect person indeed—as would Fr. Chris, Fr. Bernard, Fr. Isaiah, and a long line of other unofficial saints besides. And they would be right. The key to holiness is not strict moral turpitude but a loving, eyes-wide-open humility. They know themselves. They have a rueful familiarity with the nature of their own particular being. And they understand that whatever is happening out there because of them is not because of them at all. They are simply conduits, vehicles, and habitations for grace.

Does holiness become more possible for us as we age? I believe that in some ways it does. Many of the strong passions and desires that keep us so self-focused as young people begin to lessen as we get older. Concerns that once obsessed us, such as finding our true vocation or our destined soul mate, have long since been laid to rest. We no longer feel the need to prove ourselves at every turn. And we are less likely to engage in grandiose, self-important fantasies. In many ways, we know much better who we really are, a state more conducive to humility.

But this quieter, more acquiescent temperament does not guarantee that we'll become holy. As Cistercian monk Michael Casey points out:

> It has been noted that most of the manifestations of humility described by St. Benedict and other writers of the monastic tradition are not virtues but simply the result of slowing down that comes with old age. The young are typically active and adventurous, boisterously self-assertive, and they make a lot of noise. The old prefer their settled routines, a quiet corner, and the abandonment of all initiative and ambition.[47]

In such a state, we can easily become complacent, lazy, and amiably hedonistic, our need for comfort and security outweighing the potential for, and inclination toward, holiness.

Thus, if we are to become blessings for the world in our old age, we must still rise to meet new challenges, some of them extremely painful. We must be willing to give up old securities for new unknowns and old loves for new solitude. We must be willing to take a journey to the depths of ourselves at the very time we feel that we most deserve a rest. And we must be willing to make the same downward journey that Jesus made when he descended from the Father to the world.

Someone who took on these late-in-life challenges, albeit with enormous trepidation and a lot of attendant suffering, was the

Dutch priest Henri Nouwen. For many years a psychologist and pastoral counselor at the Menninger Clinic, he went on to a successful academic career at Notre Dame, Harvard, and Yale. A popular and prolific spiritual writer, he seemed to be at the top of his game when he first became aware of a new call—the call to give up his intellectual life and become a caregiver to profoundly disabled people in a Toronto L'Arche community called Daybreak.

He becomes excruciatingly honest with himself and his readers when he realizes, while undergoing a year-long time of preparation for his new role, that he is almost completely unsuited for what will happen next:

> Everything in me wants to move upward. Downward mobility with Jesus goes radically against my inclinations, against the advice of the world surrounding me, and against the culture of which I am a part. . . . Wherever I turn, I am confronted with my deep-seated resistance against following Jesus on his way to the cross and my countless ways of avoiding poverty, whether material, intellectual, or emotional,[48]

He worries that, until now, his "whole life has been centered around the word: learning, teaching, reading, writing, speaking. Without the word, my life is unthinkable."[49] For him, a good day is a "day with a good conversation, a good lecture given or heard, a good book read, or a good article written."[50] To live among those who are severely handicapped, many of whom cannot speak at all, he must be willing to give up what has given his life meaning. In his new community, everything is based on the body. "Feeding, cleaning, touching, holding—this is what builds the community. Words are secondary. . . . It is the language of the body that counts most."[51]

As he struggles to overcome his resistance to this different way of being, he finds himself dangerously close to despair. Though he recognizes the temptation for what it is, the urge to give up is almost too much for him. For if he lets despair do its work in him, his problems are seemingly solved. "This strangely attractive voice takes all uncertainties away and puts an end to the struggle. It speaks unambiguously for the darkness and offers a clear-cut negative identity."[52]

Yet in the midst of the struggle, he attends a Good Friday service filled with the people who will make up his new community. As a huge crucifix is taken down from the wall and held upright so that the congregants can come forward and kiss it, he has an overwhelming vision of the immense suffering of humanity:

> [P]eople killing each other; people dying from starvation and epidemics; people driven from their homes; people sleeping on the streets of large cities; people clinging to each other in desperation; people flagellated, tortured, burned, and mutilated; people alone in locked flats, in prison dungeons, in labor camps, . . . all crying out with an anguished voice, "My God, my God, why have you forsaken us?"[53]

He is filled with horror. But it is in this moment of anguish that he realizes, as if for the first time, that the love of Christ can make whole even the most profoundly fractured human beings: "I saw Jacques, who bears the marks of suffering on his face, kiss the body with passion and tears in his eyes. I saw Ivan carried on Michael's back. I saw Edith coming in her wheelchair. As they came—walking or limping, seeing or blind, hearing or deaf—I saw the endless procession of humanity gathering around the sacred body of Jesus."[54]

Nouwen goes forward, committing himself to the L'Arche community where he becomes the attendant, companion, and soul-friend to people who are profoundly mentally and physically challenged. His special charge, Adam, cannot bathe himself, dress himself, feed himself, go to the bathroom without assistance, walk, speak, or spend a day without undergoing multiple seizures. Nouwen, who has spent his life as a priest and a professor, has never had to cook for himself before, much less for others. Very quickly, he is brought face-to-face with his own inadequacy—as he puts it, with his "own handicaps."

But he stays, knowing that this stripping away of everything that once gave meaning to his life is the path to holiness for him. The outcome, if he can survive it, will be a great gift: the great privilege of blessing the world.

Several months ago, Mike, my mom, my brother, and I went to visit Uncle Ivan and Aunt Pauline. It was Christmas, snow was falling, and their senior apartment complex was decorated with lighted trees, wreathes, and holly branches. Ivan, decked out in one of his Norwegian sweaters and looking more than ever like Santa Claus, was waiting for us in the foyer. He greeted us with his usual jovial laugh, gave us warm hugs, and led us to the elevator and down the long hallway to their door. But despite his cheerfulness, I couldn't help but notice his pallor and fatigue. And when it came time to go out to dinner, for the first time that I could remember, he begged off. "Tired," he said. "Getting old is not for the weak."

When we got back to the apartment a couple of hours later, he was asleep in his easy chair, exactly where we'd left him. It was clear he had not eaten. Pauline said, a little worriedly, "He's getting this way. Lots of sleeping." All of us stood there for a moment, watching him swim back to the surface. He seemed embarrassed, as though we'd caught him somehow, as though sleeping was not in his job description. Even though it made us sad, ultimately it didn't matter to us that he was worn out or getting close to departing this world: his healing, strengthening effect was the same as it had ever been.

Fr. Chris, that lover of the Eucharist, woke up one morning last fall with leg problems. He had a hard time getting out of bed, and then—much worse—a hard time handling light. There seemed to be something wrong with his eyes. During the next three days, his symptoms grew scarily more severe. Local doctors were stumped and sent him on to Stanford. And there, after much testing, they finally determined what he had: Devic's syndrome, an extremely rare, incurable autoimmune disorder that attacks both the optic nerve and the spinal cord. Would he get better? Perhaps. But never completely. Whatever happened, he would spend the rest of his life—and he is only fifty—dealing with this radically early onset of old age, at least in terms of his physical capacity.

For a while, he was fully immersed in simply learning how to function again. And then, as the symptoms of this initial attack began to ease, he returned to Sunday Mass, this time in a wheelchair. It took several more months for him to actually walk again. Recently, glad to know that he was much improved, I went to visit him. As we sat talking in his office, I asked him what he had learned spiritually from this difficult trial.

He said, "Well, at first, when I was still paralyzed, I felt as though I were in a cage. And I didn't know what to do. I'm so used to making plans and getting things done. But then I thought, there's still one thing I *can* do, even when I'm completely helpless."

"What's that?"

"I realized that I could be loving to the people who were caring for me. I could offer them my love, even when I couldn't lift a finger to help myself."

I was gazing at him, rapt, and he shrugged and gave me an abashed smile. "And did you?" I prompted.

He nodded. "And it was one of the most beautiful spiritual experiences I've ever had. It was a kind of union with my fellow human beings unlike anything I've ever known before. I wish I could get it back now, or at least at that level of intensity." He paused, looking pensive. "It's harder now that I'm back to doing most things for myself."

Like Henri Nouwen at L'Arche, Fr. Chris now understands 2 Corinthians 12:9 on an experiential level: "My grace is sufficient for you, for power is made perfect in weakness." The confrontation with his own helplessness—which is the universal human helplessness we strive so hard to avoid acknowledging in ourselves—gave him a glimpse of the world as Christ sees it.

Departing

Aging brings us face-to-face with our own mortality. Steadily, or all at once, we begin to lose physical strength, energy, and the ability to think straight. The difficult part is that no matter how old we become, we never stop feeling like ourselves—the children we once were, the young adults who faced life with such eager hope, the parents who watched with joyful trepidation as their own children began the same journey. From where we now stand, this long trip feels heartbreakingly brief. How can it be that creatures such as ourselves, astonishing beings capable of seeing into the life of things—how can it be that we will end?

But we will end, at least in this form we have come to think of as "us." And what happens next is beyond our current ability to comprehend. For now we see through a glass darkly, says St. Paul, but only then will we see face-to-face (1 Corinthians 13:12). St. John of the Cross might call what awaits us the ultimate "oscura," that black and mysterious deep-space realm of pulsing love and light. Where we are going, we do not know. We only know that Jesus has promised to prepare for us there a new and marvelous dwelling place.

Meanwhile, we begin our long good-bye to what we have loved most. And this is never easy. It shouldn't be, for what we have loved here on earth is precious beyond compare. The parents who adored us. The stouthearted partner or best friend who has seen us at our weakest and our worst, yet still cherishes our existence. The siblings or childhood companions who have known us since we were downy-cheeked grade-school kids, arguing in the sandbox. Our own adult children, if we had them, or our admirable nieces and nephews or godchildren, tall and competent and wise and strong. Our achingly beautiful grandbabies, whether related to us by blood or simply ours through love.

We are bidding farewell to our blue and beautiful planet, with its vast seas and green forests and towering masses of light-rimmed clouds. We are saying good-bye to mountains, redwoods, rivers, herds of caribou, and pods of whales. We are letting go of the night sky and the great white lamp of the moon, the fields and fields of poppies in the spring. We are relinquishing the good work we did and the work we dreamed of doing, the thoughts we thought and the wonder we felt, the puzzles of the universe that we never solved, and the insights that flickered through our psyches like summer lightning, striking us dumb. We are leaving behind the tears that choked us as we listened to Bach or stood before a Rembrandt or read the final pages of *The Brothers Karamazov*. We are bidding adieu to the sweet, sweet happiness of perfect crème brûlée. Life, with all its sins and sorrows, has truly been a wondrous gift. As we begin to see the end approach, it's no wonder we become pensive.

As a good monk, Fr. Bernard had decades of *memento mori* behind him. If anybody was ready to die, it should have been him. Yet, as Janet and I perched beside his bed in the monastery infirmary, he seemed agitated, even distressed. There were things he still wanted to tell us, and the Parkinson's had now reached the point of making him pretty well incomprehensible. His emotions were running so high that, after one long look at each of our faces, he turned his troubled gaze to the air in front of him, speaking rapidly and breathlessly, as though he knew that time was running out, which it was.

The novice in attendance, Charbel, told us that Fr. Bernard had been this way for more than a week, trying at first to clamber out of the high bed as if he had somewhere to go. "But his legs are as weak as cooked spaghetti," said Charbel, "so he'd fall flat on the floor if we let him get up."

Janet said, "My dad was the same way. For a few days before he died, he got frantic—kept saying he had to go somewhere—and we had to get in bed with him and hold him there or he would have escaped. I wonder if men just do that."

The three of us sat there, musing. Fr. Bernard, who had fallen silent when we spoke, who was clearly still connected to his physical context albeit by a slender silken string, took up his troubled discourse once again, punctuated by another long look into each of our faces.

"Are you getting any of this?" Janet asked me.

"A little," I said. "He's worried, isn't he?"

She nodded. "He's worried about the monastery budget." The recession was finally starting to wind down, but the dearth of retreatants during the hardest months had put a major dent in the coffers. And even though he was living through his last hours on earth, this totally bugged Fr. Bernard.

"Unfinished business, maybe? Is that why guys try to crawl out of their beds like that?" It was the only thing I could think of, but I had to admit, it was a bit of a letdown. I assumed with someone as spiritually advanced as Fr. Bernard that his final moments would be filled with profound thoughts or transcendent insights or, at the very least, a vision of Jesus welcoming him home. But apparently not; what was on his mind was money.

Janet shrugged. "All I know is that after my dad went through that high-anxiety, agitated stage, he finally calmed down and got peaceful. And when he died, his face was beautiful."

And that's exactly what happened with Fr. Bernard, who passed from this world less than forty-eight hours later. When we finally took our leave of him, his pale cheeks were high with passionate color—there was more he had to say, but no more strength to say it—and all we could do was pat that beloved face, kissing it and patting it as though he were the sweetest and freshest of infants, just out of the bath. All we could do was smile at him and tell him we loved him. He'd been breathing very rapidly, nearly panting in his distress, but Fr. Bernard, even in his extremity, had no defenses against womanly affection, and so we left him beaming. When the end finally came, Charbel told us later, it was quite peaceful, a final deep sleep. Even his breaths, which had grown raggedly noisy in this last stage, calmed and grew quiet.

Who knows what he saw at the end?

My mother-in-law, Mary, went into hospice care shortly before her sixty-sixth wedding anniversary. She and Bud had moved to a local assisted living residence just months before. Family members came from everywhere to say good-bye, and, with fifteen of us in attendance, Mary suddenly woke out of the semicoma she'd been in for several weeks. She stared wonderingly around the room, then said in a perfectly clear voice, "Let us pray."

Startled, we bowed our heads as she led us through the entire Our Father. At the final "Amen," she lay back against the pillows, closed her eyes, and gave a deep, shuddering, last-breath-like sigh. Mike cried out and fell into the arms of our daughter Kelly. People began to weep out loud. Such a death, surrounded by relatives and brought to a close through the inspired words of Jesus, seemed close to miraculous. "It's just like in a movie!" someone whispered in awe.

But it wasn't. Fifteen minutes later, she woke again, this time in a state of mumbling disorientation. The relatives, who'd been filling the hallway of the residential care unit for several days by now, took this as their exit cue and left. At the moment of her actual passing, which happened nearly two weeks later, Mike was the person on watch. But I had been there earlier that day, sitting beside her in her death struggle, thinking this: *Dying is as hard as being born.*

❧

Because my friend Margaret Joy can no longer go out, except to the doctor, we meet at her place, four women she has chosen for her "team." She sits regally upright in the center of her sofa, wrapped in an elegant silk shawl the color of peaches, her narrow face festooned by the clear plastic lines that connect her to the oxygen tank. Margaret Joy, who has never smoked a day in her life, has terminal lung cancer, and we four are meant to help her through it. I can guess why she asked the others; one is a psychologist, another a physical therapist, the third a spiritual director and fierce advocate for justice, medical and otherwise. But what about me? Aside from our love for one another (but Margaret loves *many* people, I tell myself, so why me and not them?), all I can think of is that I'm here to be a witness. She needs to know what her dying looks like through the eyes of a professional observer.

I'm sad that she and Mom will never meet. Both eighty-four, they are contemporaries. Lovers of good books, good art, and good music, they might have had some things in common. But Mom moved into her new apartment in our town the month the cancer cells began to move into Margaret's lungs, and even though we went so far as to plan a tentative lunch date, Margaret was very quickly too exhausted to handle anything but the essential. And so the opportunity passed, never to return.

Today we are talking about the coming month, when Margaret's brother will fly back to the East Coast and her son will return to work in another city. "I'm still pretty good," she says. "I can get myself up in the night to go to the bathroom, and I can still putter in the kitchen when I need to. But it helps just knowing somebody is here."

What she's not saying, but what we've learned through her brother, is that she's having frightening coughing attacks, often in the wee hours, and even though there's nothing anybody can do, it comforts her to know she's not alone. So we look around the circle. Who would be willing to take a weekly shift? I know I would and so would the others. What's not being articulated is our fear of being woefully unprepared for the job. None of us is a trained caregiver. What if she falls and we need to get her off the floor? What if she can't stop coughing?

She says, "The hospice nurse thinks it's time to start some morphine." Margaret Joy hates drugs, always has, and much prefers to go to an acupuncturist when she hurts rather than take a single aspirin. But those options are closing off fast.

"How bad is the pain now?" asks one of the women. "On a scale of one to ten?"

"Most of the time, not that bad. Just a lot of pressure on my chest. But sometimes when I get those spasms around the sternum, it's an eight."

"An *eight?*"

"I do know a little something about pain," Margaret says dryly. "Trust me—it's an eight."

This is my cue. "Margaret," I say, "morphine is *great.*"

"It is?" She looks surprised. "Better than Mike's home-made wine?"

"Way better," I say. "It will send you on a spiritual adventure you will never forget."

Her son, up till now quiet in the rocking chair, snorts out loud. She starts to grin. "No kidding?"

I nod. "If it weren't so addictive, I'd be asking for prescriptions all the time." I am totally lying here, and Margaret knows it, but this, in her present moment of fear, is what she needs to hear.

"But won't *I* get addicted?"

We give each other sly looks, waiting for her to get the joke. And she will; one thing that's never happened in all the time I've known her is that Margaret fails to get the joke. "Oh," she says finally, a little abashed. "I see what you mean." Then, without warning, she starts to cry, and this is something none of us is used to seeing. Flustered but trying to hide it, we wait while she weeps into her hankie, then blows her nose. "I'm sorry," she says. "I've been a little blue."

"Of course you have," I say. "It's the long good-bye. Everybody who's been coming to see you—it's the last time, right?"

She nods, tears still leaking.

"If you didn't cry, there'd be something wrong with you," I add.

But Margaret, ever honest, can't let it rest there because that would be misleading. "I love them all, and I'm so glad to see them, and it's sad to say good-bye for the last time, true, but that's not why I'm crying."

"It's not?"

"I'm crying because it's all getting to be too much. I don't know how much longer I can be present for all this. It's overwhelming."

"You're starting to be somewhere else," says one of the women.

"I am."

"You've *always* been somewhere else, Margaret," says somebody else. "Or at least halfway."

We laugh; this is true. There's always been something ethereal about our friend Margaret. Her best pal Liz told us, before she, too, left for the last time, that throughout their many decades of friendship, she'd always had the feeling that she was holding onto Margaret's coattails to keep her from floating off into the stratosphere.

I will never stop missing her when she finally does.

Shortly after the wedding banquet during which we almost lost my Uncle Lowell, he fell again. This time he wasn't found for twelve hours. Though he survived, the delicate thread to which he'd been clinging—the spider-thin line that connected him to his own short-term memory—quietly gave way. Weakened by the ordeal and too confused to go back to the farm, he agreed to move into a memory care facility. In his room he has his bed from home, a nineteenth-century rocker he restored himself, and the one-hundred-and-thirty-year-old dresser carved by my Norwegian great-grandfather. When I talked to him last, he seemed content, telling me he was waiting for a warm day so that he could move his chair outside and sit in the sun. "I've got the spot all picked out," he said.

"What do you do with your time?" I asked him.

"I read."

"What kind of books?"

"Oh," he said. "Well, I suppose I mostly read books about clearing the land, planting crops, that kind of thing."

"About farming."

"Well, yes. Never really thought about it."

"Makes sense to me," I said.

"Well, me too," he said. "Now that you mention it."

We fell silent. I tried to imagine him two thousand miles away, talking to me from a memory care facility instead of from the small kitchen of the family farm. My childhood paradise. But it just wouldn't compute.

"I'm going to look around our house," I said, "and see what kinds of farming books we might have. How do you feel about olives?"

"Olives?"

"Well, that's what we grow here."

"You don't say," he said, sounding suddenly fascinated. "You must have quite a climate there in California."

"We do," I said. "It's quite a place. Anyway, if I find anything you might like, I'll send it to you, OK?"

"Well, that's very nice of you," he said. "And I appreciate your calling."

What I will miss most about my Uncle Lowell is this old-fashioned courtesy of his, curiously formal for such a man of the soil, but warm, too. I can always count on it, and for as long as he is with us, on him, too. And I pray that when he's getting ready to go, somebody—my cousin, my sister—will be there next to the bed, keeping watch, so that he doesn't try, like Fr. Bernard and like Janet's father, to escape.

I want him to know that somebody will be feeding his cat. That all will be well with the farm, even if it finally passes out of the family. That life, even in the face of death, is irrepressible.

That death does not end a thing.

Questions for Reflection and Small-Group Discussion

Arriving

This opening chapter talks about the social pressure we face to obtain what we most want before we die. What is it that you still long to do? How might this list be trimmed and made more realistic?

What do you think is your biggest impediment to accepting your own aging?

Chapter 1: Listening

What is your own "life story," and how does it shape the way you see the world?

What "consoling illusions" do you depend on? Do you think you might be able to let any of these go? How might you go about doing that?

What are some things you might do to be able to listen better in the spiritual sense?

Chapter 2: Delighting

Are you plagued by anxiety? If so, over what?

What gives you the most joy? Is this joy also accompanied by a certain level of anxiety? If so, why?

How might you begin delighting in something that currently makes you feel anxious?

Chapter 3: Lightening

What possessions might you shed to lighten up your life?

What is your relationship to money? Do you find yourself cheered up by spending? Are you, on the other hand, someone who finds great satisfaction in saving? What does money represent to you?

Chapter 4: Settling

Do you feel at peace in the place and the situation in which you live? If not, why not?

Is there something unfinished in your life that still pulls at you? If so, what is it?

What would it take for you to settle down where you are?

Chapter 5: Confronting

Is there something in your past that you know you need to deal with? If so, what is it?

What prevents you from facing up to it? What might help you do so?

Chapter 6: Accepting

What gives you strength? Is this something eternal and unchanging, or something material that will pass away?

Do you find yourself clinging too much to the things you love? Is there a way to love people and things without such a high degree of dependence?

Chapter 7: Appreciating

Are you aware of any inner source of anger or frustration? If so, have you ever spoken to anyone about it?

How do you think this anger or frustration might be getting in the way of your living a peaceful, happy life?

What are you most thankful for? Can you identify things you know you should be grateful for that you currently take for granted?

Chapter 8: Befriending

Have you ever been in the position of a friendless stranger? If so, did anyone help you out?

Have you ever extended yourself to someone new? If so, what was the result?

What do you think your biggest impediment to befriending others might be?

Chapter 9: Generating

What do you personally have to offer the upcoming generation?

Have you ever tried to offer what you know? If so, was your gift accepted or rejected?

Were you ever mentored by someone else? If so, what kind of effect did this have on your life?

Chapter 10: Blessing

Who in your life has blessed you simply by being there?

Have you ever met someone you believe to be holy? If so, what gave you that impression?

Leon Bloy says, "There's only one sadness, the sadness of not being a saint." What do you think he means?

Departing

Are you or anyone you love close to death at the moment? What is the hardest good-bye in this situation?

What do you think happens to us after we die? Do you find death frightening?

What do you think would be the most comforting thing people could do for you when you are dying?

Notes

1. Frank Tuoti, *Why Not Be a Mystic?* (New York: Crossroads, 1995).

2. www.griefwiththelord.wordpress.com/2011/06/13/poem-by-st-ephrem

3. Diadochus of Photikë, *Following the Footsteps of the Invisible*, trans. Clifford Ermatinger (Collegeville, MN: Liturgical Press, 2010), 74.

4. Ibid, 37.

5. Ibid., 12.

6. Ibid., 92.

7. Thomas Merton, *The New Man* (New York: Noonday Press, 1961), 5.

8. St. Nikodimos of the Holy Mountain and St. Makarios of Corinth, *The Philokalia: The Complete Text*, Vol. I, trans. and ed. by G.E.H Palmer, Phillip Sherrard, and Kallistos Ware (London: Faber and Faber, 1979), 177.

9. Ibid., 70.

10. Ibid., 60.

11. Ibid., 60.

12. Ibid., 54.

13. Ibid., 54.

14. Lisa M. Bitel, *Isle of the Saints: Monastic Settlement and Christian Community in Early Ireland* (Ithaca, N.Y.: Cornell University Press, 1990), 225–226.

15. http://en.wikipedia.org/wiki/columbanus.

16. http://www.fordham.edu/halsall/basis/bede-cuthbert.asp (quote from Chapter XVIII of Bede's *The Life and Miracles of St. Cuthbert, Bishop of Lindesfarne*), 721.

17. Bede, *Ecclesiastical History of the English People, The Greater Chronicle, Bede's Letter to Egbert,* ed. by Judith McClure and Roger Collins, Oxford World's Classics (Oxford: Oxford University Press, 1999), 223.

18. Amedee Hallier, O.C.S.O., *The Monastic Theology of Aelred of Rievaulx: An Experiential Theology,* trans. by Columban Heaney, O.C.S.O., trans. of Aelred's works by Hugh McCaffery, O.C.S.O. (Shannon, Ireland: Irish University Press, 1969), 36.

19. Ronda De Sola Chervin, *Prayers of the Women Mystics* (Ann Arbor: Servant Publications, 1992), 22.

20. Ibid., 19.

21. Ronda De Sola Chervin, *Prayers of the Women Mystics* (Ann Arbor: Servant Publications, 1992), 70.

22. Julian of Norwich, *Revelations of Divine Love*, trans. Clifton Wolters (New York: Penguin, 1966), 63.

23. Amy Frykholm, *Julian of Norwich: A Contemplative Biography* (Brewster, MA: Paraclete Press, 2010), 70.

24. Ibid., 108.

25. Ibid., 99.

26. Ibid., 55.

27. Ibid, 100.

28. http://www.ccel.org/ccel/lawrence/practice.iv.vii.html (quote from Brother Lawrence's *Practice of the Presence of God*, Seventh Letter).

29. http://www.ccel.org/ccel/lawrence/practice.iv.iv.html (quote from Fourth Letter).

30. http://www.ccel.org/ccel/lawrence/practice.iii.i.html (quote from First Conversation)

31. http://www.ccel.org/ccel/lawrence/practice.iv.vi.html (quote from Sixth Letter).

32. http://www.ccel.org/ccel/lawrence/practice.iv.xii.html (quote from Twelfth Letter).

33. Archimandrite Lazarus Moore, *An Extraordinary Peace: St. Seraphim, Flame of Sarov* (Port Townsend, WA: Anaphora Press, 2009), 213.

34. Josef Pieper, *Faith, Hope, Love* (San Francisco: Ignatius Press, 1997), 220.

35. Archimandrite Lazarus Moore, *An Extraordinary Peace*, 170.

36. Ibid., 137.

37. Ibid., 174.

38. Ibid., 198.

39. John Henry Newman, *Apologia Pro Vita Sua*, ed. by William Oddie (London: Orion Publishing Group Ltd., 1993), 112.

40. Ibid., 115.

41. Ibid., 271.

42. Ibid., 307.

43. Ibid., 307.

44. Henri J.M. Nouwen, *The Road to Daybreak: A Spiritual Journey* (New York: Doubleday, Image Books, 1990), 138.

45. *Catechism of the Catholic Church* (Ligouri, MO: Ligouri Publications, 1994), 194.

46. Olivier Clément, *On Human Being: A Spiritual Anthropology* (New York: New City Press, 2000), 138.

47. Michael Casey, *A Guide to Living in the Truth: Saint Benedict's Teaching on Humility* (Ligouri, MO: Ligouri Publications, 2001), 8.

48. Henri Nouwen, *The Road to Daybreak,* 154.

49. Ibid., 150.

50. Ibid., 150.

51. Ibid., 150–151.

52. Ibid., 157.

53. Ibid., 160.

54. Ibid., 161.

Bibliography

Armstrong, Karen. *Visions of God: Four Medieval Mystics and Their Writings*. New York: Bantam Books, 1994.

Bede. *The Ecclesiastical History of the English People, The Greater Chronicle, Bede's Letter to Egbert*. Edited by Judith McClure and Roger Collins. Oxford: Oxford University Press, 1999.

Belisle, Peter-Damian, O.S.B. Cam., ed. *The Privilege of Love: Camaldolese Benedictine Spirituality*. Collegeville, MN: Liturgical Press, 2002.

Bitel, Lisa M. *Isle of the Saints: Monastic Settlement and Christian Community in Early Ireland*. Ithaca, NY: Cornell University Press, 1990.

Bondi, Roberta C. *To Love as God Loves: Conversations with the Early Church*. Philadelphia: Fortress Press, 1987.

Boersma, Hans. *Heavenly Participation: The Weaving of a Sacramental Tapestry*. Grand Rapids, MI: Wm. B. Eerdmans, 2011.

Bornstein, Carol, David Fross, and Bart O'Brien. *California Native Plants for the Garden*. Los Olivos, CA: Cachuma Press, 2005.

Burton-Christie, Douglas. *The Word in the Desert: Scripture and the Quest for Holiness in Early Christian Monasticism*. New York: Oxford University Press, 1993.

Casey, Michael. *A Guide to Living in the Truth: Saint Benedict's Teaching on Humility.* Ligouri, MO: Ligouri Publications, 2001.

Catechism of the Catholic Church. Liguori, MO: Liguori Publications, 1994.

Chervin, Ronda De Sola. *Prayers of the Women Mystics.* Ann Arbor, MI: Servant Publications, 1992.

Clément, Olivier. *On Human Being: A Spiritual Anthropology.* New York: New City Press, 2000.

Diadochus of Photikë. *Following the Footsteps of the Invisible: The Complete Works of Diadochus of Photikë.* Translated by Cliff Ermatinger. Collegeville, MN: Liturgical Press, 2010.

Dulles, Avery. *John Henry Newman.* London: Continuum, 2009.

Egan, Harvey D. *Karl Rahner: The Mystic of Everyday Life.* New York: Crossroad, 1998.

Evagrius Ponticus. *The Praktikos and Chapters on Prayer.* Translated by John Eudes Bamberger, O.C.S.O. Kalamazoo, MI: Cistercian Publications, 1981.

Frykholm, Amy. *Julian of Norwich: A Contemplative Biography.* Brewster, MA: Paraclete Press, 2010.

Hernandez, Wil. *Henri Nouwen: A Spirituality of Imperfection.* New York: Paulist Press, 2006.

John of the Cross. *The Collected Works of Saint John of the Cross.* Translated by Kieran Kavanaugh, O.C.D. and Otilio Rodriguez, O.C.D. Rev. ed. Washington, DC: Institute of Carmelite Studies, 1991.

Julian of Norwich. *Revelations of Divine Love.* Translated by Clifton Wolters. New York: Penguin, 1966.

Lawrence of the Resurrection, Brother. *The Practice of the Presence of God.* Translated by Donald Atwater. Springfield, IL: Templegate, 1974.

Mariani, Paul. *Gerard Manley Hopkins: A Life.* New York: Viking, 2008.

Merton, Thomas. *The New Man.* New York: The Noonday Press, 1961.

Middleton, Herman A. *Precious Vessels of the Holy Spirit: The Lives and Counsels of Contemporary Elders of Greece.* Thessalonica, Greece: Protecting Veil Press, 2003.

Moore, Archimandrite Lazarus. *An Extraordinary Peace: St. Seraphim, Flame of Sarov.* Port Townsend, WA: Anaphora Press, 2009.

Murdoch, Iris. *Metaphysics As a Guide to Morals.* London: Penguin, 1993.

Newman, John Henry. *Apologia Pro Vita Sua.* Edited by William Oddie. London: Orion Publishing Group Ltd. (Everyman's Library), 1993.

Nicholl, Donald. *Holiness.* New York: Paulist Press, 1987.

Nikodimos of the Holy Mountain and St. Makarios of Corinth. *The Philokalia: The Complete Text.* Vol. I. Translated and edited by G. E. H. Palmer, Philip Sherrard, and Kallistos Ware. London: Faber and Faber, 1979.

_____. *The Philokalia: The Complete Text.* Vol. II. Translated and edited by G. E. H. Palmer, Philip Sherrard, and Kallistos Ware. London: Faber and Faber, 1990.

Nouwen, Henri J. M. *The Road to Daybreak: A Spiritual Journey.* New York: Doubleday, Image Books, 1990.

Pieper, Josef. *Faith, Hope, Love.* San Francisco: Ignatius Press, 1997.

Squire, Aelred, O.P. *Aelred of Rievaulx: A Study.* London: Cistercian Publications, 1981.

Stewart, Columba. *Cassian the Monk.* Oxford Studies in Historical Theology. New York: Oxford University Press, 1998.

The Syriac Fathers on Prayer and the Spiritual Life. Translated by Sebastian Brock. Kalamazoo, MI: Cistercian Publications, 1987.

About the Author

Paula Huston, A National Endowment for the Arts Creative Writing Fellow, has published fiction and essays for more than twenty years. She is the "cement" between generations, watching her own children parent while watching her mother face end-of-life issues. She lives in Arroyo Grande, California.

Also by Paula Huston

THE HOLY WAY
$15.95 • Pb • 1441-7

Drawing on the powerful histories
of the saints and her own personal
experience, author Paula Huston
shows us how living simply begins
with a commitment to spiritual simplicity in our lives. Each chapter in
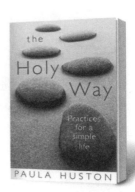
The Holy Way introduces a different spiritual practice,
including solitude, purity, and generosity, and explores
it through historical perspectives and Huston's compelling
personal reflections.

BY WAY OF GRACE
$19.95 • Hc • 2331-0

By Way of Grace is Huston's artfully
written account of what she learned
during her struggle to grow in faith
and to accept God's grace. The book
contends that the spiritual life firmly
rests on saints and virtues, and each

chapter focuses on how a great saint of the mystical
Catholic tradition explains and exemplifies one of the
traditional Christian virtues.

To order: call 800-621-1008, visit www.loyolapress.com/store,
or visit your local bookseller.

Continue the Conversation

If you enjoyed this book, then connect with Loyola Press to continue the conversation, engage with other readers, and find out about new and upcoming books from your favorite spiritual writers.

Visit us at
www.LoyolaPress.com
to create an account and register for our newsletters.

Or you can just click on the code to the right with your smartphone to sign up.

Connect with us on the following:

Facebook   **Twitter**   **You Tube**
facebook.com/loyolapress twitter.com/loyolapress youtube.com/loyolapress